Exam Stress

Other titles from Bloomsbury Education

The Emotionally Intelligent Teacher by Niomi Clyde Roberts

The Wellbeing Toolkit: Sustaining, supporting and enabling school staff by Andrew Cowley

100 Ideas for Secondary Teachers: Engaging parents by Janet Goodall and Kathryn Weston

Happy School 365 by Action Jackson

Live Well, Learn Well by Abigail Mann

Proactive Pastoral Care by Maria O'Neill

What Every Teacher Needs to Know: How to embed evidence-informed teaching and learning in your school by Jade Pearce

Leading on Pastoral Care by Daniel Sobel

Succeeding as a Head of Year by Jon Tait

Growth Mindset: A practical guide by Nikki Willis

Other titles by the same author

A Parent's Guide to Exam Stress: Practical, positive ways to support your child for GCSEs, A levels and other school assessments by Katharine Radice

Exam Stress

A practical and positive guide for teachers

Katharine Radice

BLOOMSBURY EDUCATION
LONDON OXFORD NEW YORK NEW DELHI SYDNEY

BLOOMSBURY EDUCATION
Bloomsbury Publishing Plc
50 Bedford Square, London, WC1B 3DP, UK
Bloomsbury Publishing Ireland Limited
29 Earlsfort Terrace, Dublin 2, D02 AY28, Ireland

BLOOMSBURY, BLOOMSBURY EDUCATION and the Diana logo are trademarks of
Bloomsbury Publishing Plc

First published in Great Britain, 2025 by Bloomsbury Publishing Plc

This edition published in Great Britain, 2025 by Bloomsbury Publishing Plc

A catalogue record for this book is available from the British Library

ISBN: PB: 978-1-80199-694-5; ePDF: 978-1-80199-693-8; ePub: 978-1-80199-696-9

2 4 6 8 10 9 7 5 3 1 (paperback)

Typeset by Newgen Knowledge Works Pvt. Ltd., Chennai, India
Printed and bound in the UK by CPI Group Ltd, CR0 4YY

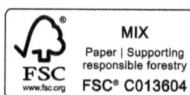

MIX
Paper | Supporting
responsible forestry
FSC
www.fsc.org   FSC® C013604

To find out more about our authors and books visit www.bloomsbury.com
and sign up for our newsletters.

For product safety related questions contact productsafety@bloomsbury.com.

Acknowledgements

Many people have helped with this book: thank you to the teachers and students who agreed to be interviewed and shared their thoughts so openly. I promised your comments would be anonymised and so I can't name you here, but you know who you are. I am so grateful to you for your readiness to be involved and the range of perspectives you brought. Thank you also to Joanna Ramsay, Amelia Mehra and the editorial and production teams at Bloomsbury for their guidance, care and attention to detail.

Thank you to the teachers who inspired me and especially to my grandmother and my mother. Thank you to my grandmother Joy for the stories she used to tell and for showing me how teaching brought her such fulfilment. Thank you to my mother Elizabeth, who has been a mentor and supporter throughout my career: you, more than anyone, have taught me the value of imagination in the classroom and the need to keep thinking about the child's perspective.

Thank you to the people who helped informally in the initial stages. Thank you to Sylvie Wright, who reminded me to be interested in the jagged edges of things. Thank you to Claire Leek, Dan Silverman and Daisy Knox for their clear-sighted feedback on the first draft and for supporting the project.

Thank you too to my family. Thank you to my father William for his interest in each new venture. Thank you to my sons, Hugo and Toby, for helping me think about what it's like to be at school today.

Thank you above all to my husband Brendan. Without you, this book would never have been possible: *you were right*.

Acknowledgment

Contents

How to use this book

Pressure at home, pressure at school, difficult exam expectations – I think it's probably a perfect storm of these things.

Assistant Head Teacher – Teaching and Learning

Why read this book?

I've been a teacher for over 20 years. I often think about what has changed in that time. I'd say that schools now are safer, kinder and more imaginative places. But I'd also say that – despite all this progress – teenagers seem much more anxious about assessments and exams. This worry about grade outcomes can impact their health, the way they work and how they behave.

I know you'll have seen this in your schools too. You'll have seen students disengage or withdraw; I'm sure you'll be able to name plenty of students who have felt so overwhelmed that they find it hard to stay in lessons or set foot in the exam hall. At the other end of the spectrum, you can probably think of students who are hyper-engaged, who listen with a taut focus, nervous about missing a beat even though they've got it nailed, their work is good and their grades seem in the bag.

For a long time I watched on from the sidelines: I was concerned about what I saw but I was mindful of the boundary lines. I'd send emails to the pastoral team, talk to my SEND or inclusion colleagues and raise it in SLT meetings, but I held back because I was a classroom teacher, not a school counsellor. Then, in 2023, I started part-time pre-clinical training to be a child and adolescent psychotherapist. I'd be in London one day, talking with mental-health clinicians about adolescent development, and then back in my classroom the next.

This blend of experience made me realise three things:

- **Development beyond the curriculum:** If a child is in a lesson, the whole child is in the lesson. While they're learning French, maths, music, etc., they are inevitably learning other things at the same time: they'll be aware of their position in the class, they'll be thinking about how others view them and their emotional dispositions will be developing concurrently with whatever it is they're learning from the school curriculum.

- **The impact of the classroom:** The reasons why teenagers are anxious are complex, and different factors will be at play in different contexts. But, whatever else is happening in the background, at school the majority of their time is spent in the classroom. When our students are stressed about their exams, there will be more to this than just what is happening in their lessons – but their experience in lessons, assemblies and form time will inevitably play its part. As teachers, we can't wave a magic wand to solve challenges in the broader context, but we can think about what's happening in our classrooms and assemblies. We can think about how changes there could help our students feel less uneasy or overloaded by exams.

- **The role of everyday adults:** Teenagers with acute anxiety need professional help. We're teachers, not mental-health professionals. There are limits to who and how we can help. But acute anxiety develops over time. Rewind the months – maybe years – and it may be the case that the acutely anxious teenager was once a bit worried, but not debilitatingly so. This book explores how we, as teachers, can understand and help teenagers who are not at the acute stage. It explores how we can be empathetic, compassionate and constructive in our interactions with young people who are feeling uneasy and who are looking to everyday adults in their lives to help them navigate these feelings.

There are many, many teenagers who feel stressed about tests and exams. After all, why wouldn't they? They're about to be judged and the outcomes are never entirely certain. It's inevitably going to cause some unease. As teachers, we can help these students. We can do this by thinking about what we are teaching them while we are teaching them maths, chemistry, history, drama and so on. We can think about the language we use and the messaging we're giving them; we can think about how we respond to the beginnings of exam stress. If we do this and help ease the stress-factors at an early stage, I hope we can also help to reduce the numbers of students who end up overwhelmed by an anxiety that has become more than they can bear.

How this book is structured

This book aims to do two things: it explores the causes of exam stress and it offers practical suggestions about how we can help.

It's structured in two parts.

- **Part 1** takes a broad overview of the causes of exam stress. Each chapter focuses on a different theme, taking key ideas and applying them to the school context. Part 1 uses material from established research in the fields of neuroscience, psychotherapy, psychology, adolescent development and cognitive science. Each chapter includes *Strategies to use*. In Part 1, these are general in nature; they relate to the messaging we give in the classroom, to year groups and during pastoral conversations. They might be useful for students at various stages in the school journey.

- **Part 2** explores how these principles apply to each of the different key stages, taking the journey through school one step at a time and offering *Strategies to use* for each area. Some of these strategies relate to what happens in the classroom; others relate to year-group assemblies or messaging to families. This is clearly signposted within each section.

As we all know, no piece of advice works equally well in all contexts. The suggestions in this book are ideas, designed to offer starting points to help you think about different approaches. You will be the best judge of how well they would work for you and your students. There is space at the back of the book for you to make notes, if you would like to.

Chapter features

- **Key takeaways:** In Part 1, you will find key takeaways boxes throughout each chapter. These summarise the most important material in each section.

- **Questions for reflection:** These are designed to help connect the material to your context.

- **Strategies to use:** Each chapter includes practical suggestions for how to make a difference in your school.

- **Areas for action:** At the end of each chapter, there is a summary of the practical suggestions.

Printable resources to support some of these strategies are available on the companion website. You can access these at bloomsbury.pub/exam-stress or via the QR code.

A range of perspectives

Throughout the book you'll hear the anonymised voices of different teenagers and adults, offering their own perspectives on exam stress.

The student voices come from young people who are either currently at school or now at university and describing their school experiences retrospectively. Their voices are central: after all, it's their experience we're trying to understand.

The adult voices belong to professionals working across the spectrum of classroom, pastoral, SEND, inclusion and mental-health provision. They range from ECTs to experienced mental-health leads and headteachers. They relay experiences in non-selective comprehensive schools, academically selective grammar schools, independent day schools, boarding schools, single-sex girls' schools, boys' schools and co-educational schools. They are taken from schools in different geographical regions of England and different socio-economic contexts, from maintained sector schools in highly deprived inner-city areas to schools with a high price-tag.

The adult and student voices belong to individuals but I've only included material that resonates with observations I've heard repeatedly in informal conversations with many others. I hope you find observations in this book that connect with your own day-to-day experience of exam stress in secondary schools.

When I was doing the interviews for his book, I was struck most of all by the following things:

- Despite the obvious differences in environments, there was remarkable consistency in the comments about how exam stress impacts young people and the causes that feed into this.

- The teachers and professionals who support teenagers are an amazing group of people: they are people who care, who keep thinking about how they do their jobs and who keep wanting to do their best by the young people they help. I left each interview feeling inspired and proud to be part of this profession.

Scope

This book takes material published by leading researchers and combines it with observations from everyday lived experience. If you would like to read further into the research that supports the generalised explanations in this book, there is a short list of suggested further reading on page 103 and a more extensive bibliography on page 183.

This book does not suggest any major changes, or require big increases in time or workload. I hope I've been realistic about what it is possible for us to do in the context of the inevitable constraints we have on our time and mental bandwidth.

My hope is that this book creates an opportunity to pause and reflect, to try to imagine ourselves into our students' experiences and to keep thinking about how best we can help them.

A note on terminology and professional boundaries

Anxious, stressed, nervous, worried: in everyday language, teenagers use a range of labels to talk about how they are feeling about assessment and exams. This is a book focused on everyday classroom practice; it aims to echo the language used in classrooms. Because of this, you will find that the terminology in this book will move between these familiar labels. This book does not use the label *anxiety* as a medical label: its focus is on how to help the students who find the prospect of assessment difficult but who are not in need of professional medical or psychotherapeutic help. Students who are suffering from anxiety as a diagnosed medical condition need help that goes beyond a classroom teacher's professional capacities.

Introduction: Why we need to talk about exam stress

My main message for school leaders? A young person who feels unhappy or unsafe is not a young person who can learn.

Education and Safeguarding Consultant

Starting points

How many students are impacted by problematic levels of exam stress? How many students in your classes do you see withdraw because they are too overwhelmed to cope? How many do you see lean in, keep working, caught in a relentless loop of trying harder to succeed? Are the numbers increasing or are we noticing it more? This book exists because I believe that we need to think searchingly about what exam stress is, why it happens and how we can help.

Why do we need to think about exam stress?

In my year group there are some acute examples of people who are working too hard – not seeing their friends etc. – and this is clearly because of their anxiety about how well they are going to do. It's hard to quantify how many – for some it's quite obvious, but for others it's harder to tell. It's hard sometimes to distinguish between who's working hard because they are motivated and who's working hard because they are anxious.

Year 11 student

The stress that some students feel about exam or test outcomes is sometimes referred to as academic anxiety. Anxiety is a state of fearfulness, felt in anticipation of a future threat (Haidt, 2024). For some students, the prospect of future assessment generates an ongoing state of unease. In 2020, Ofqual published a review of academic anxiety (Howard, 2020). It reported that anecdotal evidence and the prevalence of media interest in exam stress both suggest that it is on the rise.

In my own experience as a teacher, I have seen worry about assessment dig its claws deeper and deeper into the students I meet. I have witnessed students shake with panic during routine class assessments, grow white with nausea, leave the room because the experience feels too intolerable to endure or pick at their skin to the point of bleeding, desperate to find some release by redirecting their overwhelming feelings of panic into a tangible, visible, label-able area of physical pain.

At teaching conferences, I often hear colleagues discussing the importance of mental health in schools and especially the damaging impact of anxiety: *yes, this is a problem, yes, we need to address this, yes, this is urgent: we need to understand why our young people seem more and more frightened.* Mental-health advice websites such as the *Mental Health Foundation* echo this view: their website reports that 60% of young people aged 18–24 have felt so stressed by the pressure to succeed that they have felt overwhelmed or unable to cope (Mental Health Foundation, 2024). NHS data reports a rise in young people using NHS mental-health services in the last ten years (NHS England, 2022). In 2022–2023, anxiety was the second most common reason for referral (Children's Commissioner, 2024).

These trends can be difficult to interpret: it's possible that the rise in demands on the NHS mental-health services are the result of increased awareness about the importance of asking for help. Whatever the fine-grained truth behind the big picture is, the headlines remain clear: feeling worried is a major issue for young people today.

For a long time the tendency was to group exam stress with general anxiety: to think that some students are prone to feeling anxious in general and any signs of exam stress are symptomatic of a broader condition, best treated beyond the classroom and by mental-health professionals. Recent research, however, has argued that exam stress should be seen as something that arises from the situation students find themselves in (Cassady, 2009). This means that it can be helped by changes within the classroom and school environment.

I believe that the everyday experience in UK schools may be unintentionally fuelling the level of stress that students experience. I believe it's worth thinking about the messaging that students receive at school, the broader factors that shape their relationship with school and grade outcomes, and the neurological hard-wiring that impacts how students think and how they feel.

The good news is that – if we think carefully about all these things – we can understand the causes of exam stress better. We can then use this understanding to work out how to make positive changes.

A student who experiences any form of anxiety to an exceptional degree needs the help of medical and mental-health professionals, but this book focuses on students who are not yet at that stage. There are many, many students who are suffering from exam stress. For many of these students, their worries about exams can be eased by adapting classroom practices and through empathetic dialogue with teachers. I believe that if we can learn to help students understand their inevitable and natural exam nerves at an early stage, there is a much better chance that they do not develop into a disposition that is deeper, more problematic and harder to change.

Key takeaways

- Stress levels among teenagers seem to be on the rise.
- Many students who suffer from exam stress are not generally anxious in other areas of their lives as well; their stress is specific to the school and/or family situations they find themselves in.
- It is possible to make changes to classroom and year-group messaging in ways that significantly reduce the worry that students feel.

Questions for reflection

- How many of your students seem anxious about assessments?
- What do you think are the reasons why they feel worried?
- How much does your school talk about exam stress as something specific and separate from anxiety or feeling worried in general?

The negative consequences of stress

Feeling high levels of stress about grade outcomes can affect students in the following ways (Huberty & Dick, 2006):

- **Impact on how a student thinks:** High stress levels can affect concentration, memory, attention span and the ability to think methodically through problems.

- **Impact on how a student behaves:** High stress levels can lead to restlessness, task avoidance, erratic behaviour, irritability, withdrawal, perfectionism, failure to complete tasks or a preference for easy tasks as an alternative.

- **Impact on physical health:** Anxious students can suffer from recurrent and localised pain, raised heart rate, headaches, muscle tension, sleeping problems, nausea and vomiting.

The list makes for grim reading: exam stress can be a debilitating experience for students. What's more, students suffering from these symptoms will find it harder to work, not easier. This can create a vicious cycle: students who are worried about assessments can experience symptoms that make it harder for them to do well; this then increases their worry about the assessments.

In addition, feeling stressed about grade outcomes does not occur only during exam periods. It may hit its peak at the immediate prospect of the exam itself, but it spreads its impact more widely, affecting the choices and work habits that take place during the school year; it can also affect how a student feels about themselves afterwards. Students who are worried about outcomes are more likely to blame themselves for their mistakes and they are less likely to take the credit when they do well (Cassady, 2009).

Key takeaways

- High stress levels can affect a student's physical health.
- Feeling stressed can affect a student's ability to concentrate and think.
- Feeling worried about exam outcomes impacts how students work during the school year and how they view themselves when they get their results.

Questions for reflection

- Think about what it is like to be worried about something: how does worry make us feel? How does it impact our ability to sleep, eat and concentrate?
- When do students seem the most anxious? When do they seem the least anxious?

(cont.)

Positive or negative stress – is a stressful situation a threat or a challenge?

The stress made me focus – I need that stress to encourage me to revise.

Year 12 student

Different students experience pressure or stress in different ways and not all stress is problematic: sometimes stress has a positive effect on performance. Sometimes, stress drives engagement and spurs someone on: we often speak of *rising to the challenge*, using adrenaline to help us *bring our A-game* and so on. Talk to any head of year about strategies used to get students to engage and work hard: it's a familiar and necessary tactic to use year-group assemblies to remind students to *take their exams seriously* and tell them that *now is the moment that really matters*.

Some degree of pressure is a good thing, but the key question is what makes this pressure tip over into something negative and problematic? Crucial to whether stress brings improved or reduced performance is whether the stressful situation is seen as a challenge, offering an opportunity for success, or a threat that brings with it a risk of failure. Negative, problematic stress arises when students see a situation as a potential threat.

The threat/challenge distinction is one of the reasons why many people assume that negative stress is caused by assessments that are too difficult: it's easy to assume that if students are on track to do well, then they have nothing to worry about.

Educational theory centred on the pros and cons of difficulty has been greatly influenced by the psychologist Mihaly Csikszentmihalyi. In his work on flow, Csikszentmihalyi established the idea that optimal engagement with a task lies in the sweet spot between anxiety and boredom (Csikszentmihalyi, 1975). Within this analysis, the difficulty of the task is key: something that is too difficult will provoke anxiety but something that is too easy leads to boredom.

There is a compelling sense within this idea: challenge is needed for personal growth and we are all motivated by the buzz that comes with achievement and progress. At the other end of the scale, it's natural to be demoralised by work that is too difficult. The flow model, however, can obscure our understanding of exam stress if we assume that students will only be anxious if the task is too difficult or if we assume that maximum engagement is the holy grail of classroom success.

It's worth questioning the idea that stress only arises when material is too difficult: look around any year group and you'll see students who are anxious even when they are clearly on top of their work. It's also worth questioning the idea that all engagement is positive; in fact, for really committed students, there is often a tipping point between positive engagement and hyper-engagement, i.e. the situation where students find it very difficult to switch off and stop working.

This book will explore why assessment often triggers a threat-response by looking at external factors that lie beyond the difficulty of the test. I believe that the problem is not just the tests themselves or the relative difficulty of the tests; I believe that the following factors contribute too:

- the extent to which students believe that grade outcomes will impact or shape their lives
- whether or not students believe there is a clear and manageable route through the exams
- the extent to which students believe they are able to meet the expectations of others
- the extent to which students believe that their decisions are sensible and they are working hard enough.

Teachers often big up the importance of GCSEs because they want us to do well. I know that if things go badly at GCSEs, this isn't the end of the line. But at school no one ever says this. GCSEs are often an example teachers use for something very important – back in Year 9, if someone said, 'Why are we learning this?', the teacher would say 'Because it'll be in your GCSE'. For lots of people, this means that they might end up thinking exams are more important than they are.

Year 10 student

I think what our people don't have here is a safety net: in less-deprived areas there's a safety net – they can think if this all goes wrong, I'll be OK. It doesn't feel like that here. There's no safety net here. There's nothing to rely on beyond yourself and your own efforts. This is a huge source of pressure in schools like ours. No one here has internalised the message that if it all flops it'll still be OK. We have kids here who will probably be in prison in a year's time. Their safety net is already criminal gangs: if they leave here with nothing, that's what they have left.

Assistant Head Teacher – Teaching and Learning

Exam anxiety spreads across this school, but this is quite an academic school. I think it is worse in students who are more academic because it's more tied to who they are as a person. It's part of why they are given praise. All their lives it's been part of who they are. The risk levels tied to not being academically successful are much higher for them because their whole sense of self is tied up with this.

Counselling and Mental Health Lead

I've never gone into an exam feeling like I've done enough.

Year 13 student

Key takeaways

- A stressful situation that is viewed as a challenge provides an opportunity for growth.
- A stressful situation that is viewed as a threat can cause students to feel anxious.
- Whether or not a student views an assessment as a challenge or a threat does not only depend on the difficulty of the assessment.
- Not all engagement is positive: it is possible for a student to hyper-engage and work too hard.

Questions for reflection

- What helps a student view an assessment as a challenge, not a threat?
- What makes a student worried about assessments even if they know they are likely to do well?
- What are the downsides of working too hard?

Exam stress in high-attainment students

It is natural to assume that students worry about a test if they think it is going to go badly. This is true enough: nobody skips into the exam room with a spring in their step if they think they are going to fail. But it does not mean that students will only worry about a test if they think it is going to go badly. Negative stress can impact students from across the attainment range, including the students who are most likely to get the top grades.

In the research published about academic anxiety, however, there is often surprise that the most highly achieving students can feel anxious about academic outcomes. This is often matched in our everyday responses: *They've got nothing to worry about! If anyone is guaranteed an A-grade, it's them!*

In 2023, the Cambridge University student-counselling services reported that the most common issue brought to them by students was low self-esteem and the worry about their degree outcomes that often accompanies this. I attended a training session led by the university counselling team: when they mentioned this fact, a ripple of surprise went around the room. At face value, the situation does seem surprising: students who have made it to Cambridge are by definition academic high-flyers. The natural response is *Really? These students know that they are right at the top end of academic success – why would so many of these high-achieving students be wracked with doubts that they are not doing well enough? Don't they realise how clever they are?*

The stress felt by highly successful students sometimes goes unnoticed. The high-attainment students may not be on watch-lists for grade outcomes, but we do need to be alert to how stressed they might be. This is because:

- Grade outcomes are a core part of their identity: ambitious students really care about the grades that they get. This means that the stakes are high, emotionally, even if it is very likely that they will succeed.

- Seeming surprised that highly achieving students are worried can make it harder for these students to talk about, understand and soothe their feelings.

- Ambitious students often stay in formal education for longer and seek more challenging qualifications: this means that they go through repeated rounds of more and more challenging assessments. This can create a cycle where stress becomes habituated and harder to change.

- There is an overlap between worry about doing well enough and perfectionism (Sharfran et al., 2018): feeling worried about outcomes can drive high-attainment students to develop a perfectionist relationship with work, leading to hyper-engagement or procrastination. It impacts how students can work when they move to more challenging academic programmes. It can also spread – problematically – into other areas of their lives.

There's an invasiveness to the feeling of academic perfectionism – sort of like a non-native invasive plant, it ends up seeping into other parts of your life which were once completely unaffected, such as not being able to keep up a hobby if you're not amazing at it immediately or feeling overwhelmed or like your whole evening is ruined if you don't get into bed at the time you had planned to.

University student

Key takeaways

- High levels of exam stress are often felt by ambitious and high-achieving students.
- It is easy to feel surprised that high-achieving students feel anxious about assessments.
- Exam-related stress can cause long-term problems for high-achieving students.

Questions for reflection

- Which students seem most worried about assessments?
- Do you hear families, colleagues or other students express surprise when high-achieving students feel worried about assessments?
- Why do you think high-achieving students feel worried even though they know they are likely to do well?

A UK-based picture

Evidence gathered by the Programme for International Student Assessment (PISA) suggests that there is something very specific taking place in the UK's school systems that is generating high levels of stress and worry.

PISA evaluates education systems every three years: their 2015 report (OECD, 2017) surveyed 15-year-olds across 72 countries. On average, students from the UK reported feeling more anxious about studying and assessments than the global average: in the data for the UK, 72% students said they felt anxious about studying, in comparison to an average of 56%. In addition, 52% of UK students said they felt tense while they studied, a result that was 15% higher than the global average of 37%. Similar trends appeared in the 2018 and 2022 surveys: in 2018, the UK was among the lowest-scoring countries for academic resilience (OECD, 2019a) and students were more likely to feel miserable and worried than the global average (DfE, 2019). In 2022, 6/10 UK students reported frequent problems in motivating themselves to work independently (OECD, 2023b).

Significantly, however, higher levels of anxiety in the UK did not correlate with similarly increased levels of worry that it would be difficult to take the test (62% for the UK versus 59% for the global average (OECD, 2017)). This suggests that the causes of exam stress are not just the difficulty of the test or the perceived difficulty of the test. What's more, it invites the question of whether there are causal factors that arise directly from the everyday UK school experience. This book will explore what these might be, by looking at the assessment structure and teaching approaches generated by our public examination system. I will explain why I believe that increasingly rigid mark-scheme expectations and a culture of talking about the test on a daily basis are significant factors in the growth of exam stress.

> I can remember science lessons in Year 7 where we were being taught how to draw graphs and we were told about what would happen in the GCSE exam – we'd have to draw it within half-a-square accuracy. I didn't really have any concept of GCSEs then and suddenly they were in view. By Year 9 it was pretty frequent – probably at least one reference to the exams each day. By Year 11 it was unusual for there to be a lesson where GCSE exams didn't get mentioned. There's an unintended impact of this – hearing about them every day makes it seem like they are the most enormous thing.
>
> Year 12 student

Current advice about how to reduce exam stress

Most of the advice available for exam stress focuses on things that the individual student can do, rather than changes that schools and teachers can make. A quick survey of some of the most well-used advice websites for young people and their families – sites such as those created by the NHS, Childline, Student Minds, Mind, The Student Room, BBC Bitesize, YoungMind or the advice given by Ofqual and individual exam boards – shows that there is a remarkable consensus about the best things for a stressed-out teenager to do. Broadly speaking, this advice has four dimensions:

- **Physical health:** Taking time to sleep properly, eat well and exercise are ways to improve physical health, thus reducing the physical impact of stress.
- **Mental health:** Students are advised to talk to others; this is a way for them to understand their own feelings better and it allows them to reach out for support from trusted others.
- **Positive mindsets:** Reframing the relationship with school work is often suggested as a way to change the behavioural patterns that accompany

exam stress. Advice such as the Ofqual guidance for students encourages students to rethink their relationship with work, taking negative thoughts such as *I am rubbish at maths* and reframing them more positively, e.g. *Even if I will never be the best at maths, I will do better if I have a revision plan and stick to it* (Ofqual, 2023).

- **Approaches to studying:** Making revision plans, revising in bite-sized chunks, setting targets – this advice aims to help students with how they are working in the run-up to exams.

There is no doubt that this advice is sound, but it can be very difficult for students to follow. High levels of stress make it harder to sleep well and eat well, and it can be difficult for students to talk about how worried they feel. The situation is made more complex for students because there's often a tension between the generic pastoral advice about how to calm down and the separate exam-focused advice to *take the exams seriously because they matter.*

> *There's quite a lot on mental health in assemblies and PSHE lessons, self-esteem, coping strategies, what to do with negative thoughts, but no one at school talks about academic anxiety specifically. We're told to make sure we're not working too hard and we're looking after ourselves, but we get vastly more on the theme of* you've got to be working seriously for the exams.
>
> Year 11 student

> *Lots of teachers don't mean to put pressure on us, but there are a lot of mixed messages – teachers say exams don't really matter, but we should do lots of revision anyway.*
>
> Year 9 student

In addition, the advice to reframe the perspective often seems like it is directed at students who are not succeeding academically. It is easy for an ambitious student to ignore it or to believe that reframing their perspective means reducing their aspirations; understandably, the most ambitious students are often reluctant to do this. For the ambitious student, the advice about what to do if *they feel rubbish at maths* doesn't seem to apply to them. When it comes to study habits, the advice to make a revision plan skates over the fact that making choices, deciding what to focus on and what to leave out is a core part of what makes students anxious in the first place.

The practical advice contained in this book

This book aims to address some of the difficulties teenagers face in taking steps to make their feelings of worry more manageable. The *Strategies to use* centre on the following things:

- how we – as teachers – can facilitate constructive conversations about pre-exam nerves
- how we can help students to feel more confident in their decisions about revision and work habits
- how we can make changes in our classroom and pastoral messaging that reduce the likelihood of problematically high levels of stress developing
- how we can communicate effectively with families to help them understand better how to support their children's journey through school.

Introduction

PART 1

Understanding the causes: Strategies to help

1 Fear

> I think what does help is knowing that it is hard and it is scary but it will end. You have to accept this. I say this to people I know who are Year 11 right now. I think it's more helpful to hear that your feelings are valid and that you're not crazy for feeling that way: it is bad, but there will be an end to it.
>
> University student

Starting points

Anxiety, stress, worry: these familiar labels all refer to a subset of fear. Fear is raw and primal: it arises from some of our most hard-wired automatic response systems in the brain. It is not something we get to choose, and – when a student is really in its grip – it can feel overwhelming. This chapter will explain how we can help students understand and talk about their exam stress. It will also offer ideas for how to help students feel better when they do start to talk about how worried they are feeling.

Why talking about fear can be difficult

> When I get really stressed about tests at school, it feels like I'm lying down and there's something really heavy on my stomach. It feels like my breathing is more laboured.
>
> Year 9 student

Fear is a big label: there's an understandable expectation that it only applies to situations that are manifestly dangerous. Part of the problem in understanding and talking about exam stress is that the situations that trigger it do not seem obviously dangerous enough: *but it's only a test, you'll be fine, you don't need to worry*.

Sometimes teenagers don't want to admit they feel scared, saying things instead like *this test is stupid – I don't care what I get*. Sometimes they water down their description or deny the validity of their feelings: *it's OK really, I'm just feeling a bit worried; it's silly – I don't know why I'm feeling like this; yeah, I know it's only a test*.

Fear is often hard to verbalise or make sense of because it is generated by aspects of the brain that are operating in a way that we do not consciously pick up on. Sometimes, the cause of the fear isn't what is immediately visible: it probably isn't getting 17/20 in a maths test as a stand-alone event. Instead, what drives the fear behind exam stress can be:

- how grades shape perceptions of self-worth
- how grades impact whether or not the student will please others, especially the people whose support and love they rely on
- whether or not their marks allow the student to be the person they have been told they are supposed to be.

The *Strategies to use* at the end of this chapter will explore how to help students understand and talk about their feelings.

Key takeaways

- The symptoms of stress arise from the brain processes that relate to fear.
- It can be difficult to understand why we are afraid, especially when the situation does not seem particularly dangerous.
- When students are nervous about grades, this feeling often arises from something more than just their grade in the assessment.

Questions for reflection

- Think about a student who is worried about exams: what do you think they are worried about beyond the grade itself?
- Do the students you teach find it easy to explain why they are so worried? When they do try to explain it, what reasons do they give?

Understanding fear – the neuroscientific view

A distinction is often made between the parts of the brain that generate our rational, conscious thoughts and the parts of the brain that generate emotional or impulsive responses. Emotional or impulsive reactions emerge within us before we have a chance to think about them or consciously choose them. This way of looking at the brain aligns with our centuries-old intuitive understanding that we are driven by head and heart and that sometimes these pull us in different directions.

The tripartite model of the brain

In the 1960s, neuroscientist Paul McLean developed a tripartite model of the brain. It is a useful way to understand the different regions within the brain, their roles and the ways in which they function.

- The oldest, deepest part of the brain is the ancient animal brain, located in the brain stem. It's often referred to as the reptilian brain. It's the first part to develop and it is responsible for the most basic bodily processes needed for staying alive: breathing, blood circulation, eating, sleeping and so forth.

- Above this is the limbic system, an area often referred to as the mammalian brain. This area gives us the capabilities needed to exist in groups and to care for others. It is responsible for emotional responses, it deals with non-verbal communication and it aims to keep us safe. Within the mammalian brain is the amygdala, the area of the brain that scans sensory input for any sign of danger.

- Last to develop are the areas of the brain that contain the capacities for rational, conscious thought. The prefrontal cortex allows us to use language and to think about a situation in a way that is complex, allows for contradictions and requires considered choice-making. This area of the brain accounts for only 30% of the brain mass inside our skulls. Developmentally, it's the last area to come online and it's also the first area to shut down in times of acute stress (van der Kolk, 2014).

The brain's threat-response system

If the amygdala detects danger or some sort of threat to our safety, stress hormones – cortisol and adrenaline – are released, bringing with them raised blood pressure, increased heart rate and oxygen intake. This prepares us for our pre-programmed fight or flight survival response. All of this is useful if you suddenly have to run from a lion, but it's not great for anyone who is trying to think their way methodically through some difficult maths. To make matters worse, the hierarchy within the brain means that if the stress is severe, the emotional side of the brain starts to dominate. Brain scans show that in extreme situations the frontal lobes go off-grid and shut down (van der Kolk, 2014). When we are truly in fear for our safety, it becomes nearly impossible to think rationally about anything.

The importance of re-establishing calm

Our automatic, pre-programmed responses to stressful situations generate a decrease in conscious, rational functioning and a very altered physiological state. This is the reason why so much of the advice for anxiety or panic centres around calming down the physical reaction first: deep breathing, mindfulness and other relaxation techniques are all designed to calm the body and thus reassure the emotional side of the brain that physical safety has been restored. At that point – in theory – it becomes possible for rational brain function to return.

All this means that – for the students who are worried about exams – there is a frustrating conflict between their brain's automatic response to stressful situations and the brain-functioning needed to emerge from that situation safely. Stress responses help us run faster and for longer, but they do not help us sleep well, think calmly or maintain a balanced perspective. For the student preparing for public exams, this stress response might produce the adrenaline needed for an extra energy boost, but if it tips over into too strong a response, the stress hormones released are more likely to hold the student back from the very things that are needed for effective preparation and good grades.

If we want to help adolescents feel less worried, we need to understand what will help them feel safe. Dr Bessel van der Kolk is a world expert on trauma, fear and safety. He offers a useful analysis of how we restore feelings of safety (van der Kolk, 2014). The idea that fear generates a fight-flight-freeze response is now a well-known one, but it is also – he argues – an oversimplification. In fact, he says, our natural response to threat moves through three phases:

- **Stage 1:** We seek social engagement, i.e. we turn to others for help.
- **Stage 2:** We prepare to deal with the threat on our own: this is the fight or flight response.
- **Stage 3:** We freeze and enter a state of near collapse, preserving only the functioning that is most essential to basic physical survival.

If we can make sure that Stage 1 – social engagement – is enough, we reduce the likelihood that the brain's threat-response ramps up into the physiologically driven, stress-hormone-soaked fight or flight mode. *Talk to others* is centre-stage in the standard advice about exam stress. Doing this, however, isn't always easy: as this chapter will explore, it can be very difficult for a teenager to verbalise their exam stress. It can also be difficult for the adults in their lives to notice it in the first place, especially if they are a student who usually gets good grades or a student who says that they *just don't care.*

> I had a Year 11 student who underperformed because of her exam stress. Her parents said she'd been physically sick on the days she'd had exams. I had no idea this was happening and this was someone I taught for two subjects. I think her exam stress wasn't visible in the classroom because her mocks had been OK. Her work tailed off a bit in the summer term but the general view was she's really clever, she'll pull it together at the end. On the face of it, the exam stress looked just like she wasn't putting the effort in.
>
> Early career teacher

Key takeaways

- We have an instinctive, pre-programmed threat-response system.
- The threat-response system is initiated by the amygdala; this is part of our non-verbal brain.
- A high-level threat-response can make it harder to think rationally about anything.
- Feeling anxious about exams can make it harder to perform well in the assessment.
- The best way to help a nervous student is to help them feel safe before their fear-response becomes too intense.
- As herd mammals, we naturally look to others to help reassure us: talking to others is the best way to do this but it can be difficult for teenagers to talk about their fear.

Feeling safe within a group

One of the most important discoveries in the 1990s neuroscience revolution came in 1994, when a group of Italian scientists, led by Giacomo Rizzolatti, discovered mirror neurons. These create our ability to copy others, to empathise and to mould ourselves into groups with a shared identity and patterns of behaviour. This ability to copy others is so fundamental to our interactions that it is one of the very first things a baby can do and – importantly – the reactions of others are one of the first things that a baby looks for as reassurance of its safety (Music, 2024). If you are interested in seeing how important this is, the still-face experiment – devised by psychologist Ed Tronick – gives a rapid depiction. Easily available on YouTube, the still-face experiment offers videos of a baby's reaction when the adult becomes unresponsive to the baby. In many of the videos, the baby's near-instant disintegration into some form of distress is heartbreaking to watch, and an important reminder of how much our sense of safety and wellbeing often depends on connections to and the responsiveness of others.

The relevance of this to exam stress is that our need for the safety that comes from being in a group cuts two ways.

- The response of others is central to restoring a sense of safety; this is why the *Strategies to use* in this chapter focus on how teachers can help when students are ready to talk about their exam stress.
- Feeling secure within social and family units is essential for not feeling frightened in the first place.

One of the reasons why assessment can be so stressful for adolescents is that school grades are one of the ways that someone's value or status within a group gets defined. For a teenager facing a school exam, the risky outcome is not just the grade itself, it's the risk of disrupting the sense of self-within-a-group that comes with it. Over the years, when I have sat down with anxious students, talking through with them why they are worried about tests, they have often framed their feelings by referring to how others perceive them. I've frequently heard things like *everyone just thinks I'm stupid* or *I'm supposed to be the clever one, everyone expects me to do well* or *it's not the result that I mind – it's the way that my friends act so surprised.*

Grade outcomes are not only about marks on a bit of paper: in a system where self-definition comes wrapped up in a CV or a UCAS application, school grades are also a matter of identity. Grades impact the feelings of security that are tied to our sense of stability within a group.

> *There's the pressure of peers and teachers and how they'll get judged at home. Everyone's always being judged for what they do or how well they do. After an assessment, everyone wants to know what you got. If you're someone who likes to do well, getting a bad result makes you feel like a core part of your identity is being challenged.*
>
> Year 10 student

> *If I could sum up my academic experience, it would be the feeling of not being enough. This comes from my self-imposed pressure and my sense that other people will be disappointed in me if I don't fulfil their concept of my potential.*
>
> University student

Key takeaways

- We copy the reactions of others and we look to others for reassurance.
- We need a stable identity within our groups in order to feel safe.
- Grades affect how teenagers feel about their sense of self within a group.

Talking about fear

Perhaps counterintuitively, talking to others can have its most transformative impact if it takes place at an early stage, when the student is feeling maybe just a bit nervous about a low-stakes test. This is why Part 2 of this book starts with Key Stage 3, exploring how we can help students embed a healthy relationship with assessments before big public exams are on the horizon. If this doesn't happen, there is a risk that the nerves escalate as students move through school and the exams become more important. Exam stress that builds over time brings with it increased physical symptoms and embedded emotional habits that are much harder to recalibrate. Talking to others about exam stress, however, isn't always straightforward.

Difficulty #1: Can teenagers put fear into words?

Understanding and talking about exam stress can be difficult for a student to do. This is especially true at an early stage for at least three reasons.

- Putting feelings into words is difficult: emotions arise from non-verbal parts of the brain. Turning these into a labelled concept isn't easy.

- It can be hard to admit to feeling frightened. Nerves about low-level tests often seem out of place: a geography test – on the surface – doesn't seem dangerous enough to generate some form of fear.

- The broader causes of exam stress are complex: our instinctive needs to be part of a group, to maintain a steady identity and to meet the expectations of others – all of these belong to the mammalian part of the brain, which doesn't deal with language at all. It's entirely unrealistic to expect that an 11-year-old who feels a bit sick about school exams could understand the roots of this reaction, buried so deep as they are within our instinctive, mammalian selves. It's no surprise that children often say *I don't know why I'm feeling like this*.

Difficulty #2: Fear spreads

Understanding the structure of the brain and the role of mirror neurons also helps us to understand another important dimension to fear: it's contagious.

The contagious nature of fear can move stress levels up a gear. School tests, public exams – these take place for a cohort of adolescents all at the same time. Whatever one student might have felt independently, their response will be shaped partly by reverberations between their mirror neurons and the feelings of the people around them. By the time GCSEs are imminent, the consequences can feel immovably real, and especially so for teenagers in contexts where good grades offer the clearest route to a better life. Fear of how families will react can be very powerful, even at a young age. I have taught many students who very clearly fear their families' reactions: they fear punishment or the prospect that their families will be angry or disappointed: *you've let me down again, you should have tried harder, what's going to happen to you now? Why can't you do as well as your cousin?*

> *I've worked in this area for 24 years – we get a real mix – there is a lot of deprivation but levels vary. On the whole, most of our parents want their kids to do well – they are often first or second generation immigrants – they believe that education will help their child improve their life chances. There's a real push for their kids to do well in education.*
>
> Assistant Head Teaching & Learning

For adolescents managing the run-up to exams, the feelings they are navigating are not just their own. If a teenager opens up about their feelings to their friends, there's always a risk that their mirror neurons pick up on the worry that the other person is feeling too. There's a risk that the conversation feeds their nervousness rather than eases it. This is why conversations with calm and pragmatic teachers are an important part of helping students reduce their exam stress.

> *When I see other people who are very stressed, it makes me more stressed – I think why aren't I more stressed about the thing they're freaking out about?*
>
> Year 12 student

Difficulty #3: *You don't need to worry* – does this help?

Many of the *Strategies to use* in this book focus on the words that we say to students. This is because when students do try to talk about their worries, the standard adult responses sometimes unintentionally close the conversation down.

When I look back over my interactions with worried students, my first response always used to be *you don't need to worry*. As a herd species, we're pre-programmed to help and reassure others. *You don't need to worry* is ingrained in our speech patterns almost as deeply as greeting someone else with a friendly *how are you?* The intention behind the reassurance is good, but what it implicitly says to the child is that the situation does not warrant fear. It does not encourage them to verbalise and understand their feelings better or to ask for help the next time.

The second standard response – *just do your best* – also runs the risk of an unfortunate set of implications: if you try hard enough, you won't need to worry. The suggestion here is that feeling anxious is the result of not trying hard enough. Viewed this way, it's not surprising that exam stress can lead to problematic levels of hyper-engagement and working too hard. It's also a bit unspecific. It ignores one of the hardest things in the mix: for the student who is overwhelmed and disengaged, it doesn't help them with what to do or how to do it.

> *If you feel strong in your knowledge, then the exam feels better – so you feel that if you work harder, then it'll be less stressful.*
>
> Year 12 student

The third standard response – especially to high-attainment students – is *you'll be fine – I'm sure you'll ace it!* Again, the intention is kind, but the suggestion behind this is that security is indeed tied up with good grades; it says things will be fine because it's going to go well. It's pretty much the opposite of saying *maybe you're worried you will disappoint someone; it's natural to feel uneasy about this. But even if your grades aren't good, you'll still be the same person, you'll still be loveable. In the long run, grades define you less than it feels like right now.*

Our auto pilot responses to a younger person who is upset are influenced by the most basic, earliest interactions between adults and infants. When a young child is upset, the role of the adult carer is shaped around making things better. It's no surprise that when a secondary-school-aged child is nervous about assessment, the most natural response is to bat the fear away: *don't worry, it'll be fine*. We want to make it better, to reassure the child that there is no need to be frightened at all.

The problem is that by the time a child is a teenager, fear arises from things which are integral to our experiences as herd-living mammals. There's always judgement. We are always going to be anxious about moments that lead to some sort of definition or shifting of the hierarchy. There are always going to be moments when an adolescent feels at risk of not being enough. We need to accept that some degree of fear is inevitable and focus on helping young people learn how to understand and move through these feelings. We need to be honest about the realities of fear rather than jumping in too quickly with an unfulfillable suggestion that there's no need to be worried at all.

Fear

Key takeaways

- It can be difficult for students to understand that feeling nervous about a school test is often about something much deeper than just the test.

- Students can end up feeling anxious because others around them are stressed.

- *You don't need to worry, you'll be fine, just do your best*: these are responses that can make it harder to talk about or understand exam nerves.

- We need to help teenagers understand that some degree of fear is inevitable and help them learn how to manage it.

Questions for reflection

- Think about automatic reactions: what do you typically say to a student when they are worried?

- Think about what is said and what students hear: are these the same thing?

- What messages does your school give about exam stress? Does it help students understand why it's natural to feel worried about exams?

Strategies to use #1: Empathy

It's important to remember that when emotions are high, the rational brain can't really get a word in edgeways. We need to soothe the emotions first, create the space for the rational brain to come back online and then look for solutions.

Soothing the emotions sometimes requires physical interventions such as deep breathing techniques, designed to calm the body down, and it often requires empathy or consolation. Many people find comfort when someone can sit alongside them in our feelings. *Don't worry, it'll be fine* is a response that implicitly devalues the fear, suggests it's not necessary and tells the child to get rid of it. It brings with it the risk that the child ends up feeling that they are in some way at fault for a set of inappropriate emotions, and it can leave them feeling alone in their emotions.

I'm not surprised you are nervous – it's natural to be worried, lots of people feel this way: this is a very different response. Being alongside an adult who is unsurprised by the feeling allows the teenager to feel much calmer. The mirror neurons fire up and the brain starts to echo the other person's calm.

I do a lot of training with teachers in active listening: whatever the young person says, the first thing to do is to validate the feeling, e.g. say something like I can see that you are really anxious or I can hear that you are really worried right now. It's important to acknowledge what the child has said – not to push it away too fast by offering a solution. Listening without judgement: this is so important – it means don't offer a solution straight away. This shuts down the conversation. Children need the space and time to talk things through.

Child and Adolescent Psychotherapist

Strategies to use #2: Developing understanding

Name it to tame it is probably a familiar tag line, designed to help adolescents manage their feelings (Siegel, 2021). Naming a feeling allows someone to re-engage the verbal, rational parts of the brain. This helps the brain to balance its emotional, more impulsive responses with the more moderating force of a conscious, rationally chosen response.

When a teenager is able to understand their feelings better, their emotions seem less surprising and less overwhelming. In addition, understanding that feeling anxious is fairly inevitable in certain situations helps the teenager realise that their response is indeed tied to that situation. It helps them realise that feeling anxious is not their fault and that it will pass as the situation changes.

Sometimes teenagers need an adult's help in understanding that:

- it is natural to feel anxious even if the assessment is likely to go well.
- it is natural to feel anxious about surprising or disappointing others.
- it is natural to feel like exam grades are part of their identity.
- their feelings about their test results are real and valid right now, but will change over time.

I also think that everyday interventions are important: classroom teachers can make a difference through the language that they use. It's almost a matter of scripted responses – these can be really effective. If you're teaching a class of 30, no

Strategies to use #3: Practical next steps

Once emotions have been soothed and understood, it's time to help the student with what to do next. The key thing here is that suggestions need to be manageable and specific. For example:

- **Take a break**: Laughing, relaxing, distraction – these are things that ease the physical consequences of stress hormones. *Take time off* is familiar advice, but it really helps teenagers to have a framework for this. Giving guidelines that show teenagers how and when to take time off can help them feel that it is OK to stop working. For example: *Make sure that you do something each weekend that has nothing to do with school work. Watch 30 minutes of TV every evening that will make you laugh or relax, even if you haven't finished the work you intended to do.*

- **Tell me about something important to you that isn't this test**: Extra-curricular activities, spending time with friends, exercise – these all help keep test results in proportion, reminding the student that their grades are just one part of their life: it's not all about the test. *Tell me something you're going to do this evening that has nothing to do with school work. Tell me what you like about it or what value it has for you.*

- **Let's get specific about how you're going to prepare for the test**: Students need help in thinking in a specific and realistic way about revision. You can help them by structuring this conversation: *let's put some boundaries in and come up with a plan about what to do, when and for how long. Let's be realistic about what it's possible to do right now. Let's focus on today; dealing with the grades is tomorrow's story. We'll deal with that then.*

Every student has different levels of stress and they are aiming for different grades, so what they need to do to alleviate their stress levels will be different for everyone.

Thinking about what to do next is the essence of making a plan. This is frontline advice in the Ofqual guidance for students about exam stress (Ofqual, 2023), it's there on the websites for BBC Bitesize, the Student Room, Student Minds and so on, it's everywhere: make a plan, meet your targets, then make a new plan. Making a plan allows someone to take ownership of a situation, to find solutions and to grow in their sense of their own strength. It's the most important factor that allows a stressful situation to be an empowering challenge rather than a debilitating, fear-inducing threat. But it's also much more difficult to do than sometimes we acknowledge. Helping students with the specifics about how to make a plan can be transformative. Chapter 2 will explore how and why this is.

Areas for action

If one of your students is noticeably anxious about an assessment, remember the following principles.

- If a student seems to be getting overwhelmed by what they are feeling, focus on helping them calm their physical reactions down with slow, deep breathing. Remember that they will take their lead from others: role-model calm, gentle behaviour. Always follow up on any concerns by reporting them to pastoral leads, following your school safeguarding and wellbeing policies.
- Students often need to calm their feelings down before they can talk about them. If you notice a student is worried and doesn't seem able to talk there and then, offer them the chance to come and talk about it later: *how about you come back and see me at lunchtime so that we can check in then about this?*

(cont.)

Fear

Areas for action (*cont.*)

- If a student opens up about their feelings, help them understand what is happening. Ask them about their feelings and why they think they are feeling that way; don't close the conversation down by telling them not to worry. Offer them the labels that will help them talk about their brain and body's reactions; help them to understand why these feelings happen.
- Keep a focus on a practical and positive next step. Don't overwhelm students by talking about all the things they can do over the next few weeks: focus on the most sensible thing to do next.

2 Agency, responsibility and self-blame

The thing that's changed now is the relationship with the guilt – I've finally learned that if I try, then whatever that looks like, that's fine.

University student

Starting points

Agency means our capacity to make something happen. It's a key ingredient in the exam stress mix. Students need to believe in their ability to generate positive outcomes but this can easily tip into difficult feelings of self-blame if things go wrong. This chapter will explore how we can help students develop a nuanced understanding of agency and responsibility in a way that allows them to feel empowered in their decisions and clear in their choices.

Why do we need to think about agency?

School exams are stressful. Agency seems to have a key role in how this stress impacts students: research into academic anxiety puts agency into pole position when it comes to making sure that a stressful situation is perceived positively as a challenge, not negatively as a threat (Cassady, 2009): students are far less likely to experience negative stress if they are good at:

- making plans
- meeting their own targets
- feeling confident in their ability to work out how to succeed.

At first glance, therefore, the route map out of problematic stress seems obvious: if we help students develop their belief in their own agency, they will find exams an easier experience to navigate.

There are, however, two challenges within this:

- UK students display comparatively low belief in their academic agency. The degree to which students believe in their ability to drive their own progress seems to vary across different countries. In the 2018 PISA analysis, the UK was one of the countries where students reported the lowest confidence in their ability to work out how to succeed. Chapter 5 will offer some suggestions as to why.

- Agency is a mixed bag. The obvious benefits of making a plan can mean that that we are a bit simplistic in our thinking: it's a good idea to make a plan *full stop*; making a plan means that someone will feel more in control, more secure, less anxious *full stop*; making a plan is the answer. *Full stop*. The *obviously a good idea* nature of making a plan can mean that sometimes we don't pause to consider the problematic difficulties that lurk in the shadows. We need to think about what these difficulties are.

The difficulties of making a plan

There are five key difficulties involved in making a plan:

- **The targets need to be realistic.** Some of the most difficult conversations I've had with families have centred around the message that *just work harder* is not always the answer. If the goal is unrealistic, the plan will be equally unrealistic.

- **Agency is more limited than we like to admit.** Whatever a student does, there will always be external factors that they cannot control: no plan caters for every eventuality.

- **Agency brings with it responsibility and the dark side of responsibility is blame.** Believing that solutions can come from within is great, empowering and motivating but the logical implication of this mindset is that if a student doesn't succeed, then it is their fault. Underpinning exam stress is often the fear of retrospective self-blame and the internal anger of *I should have done things differently*.

- **Making choices about revision is complicated.** The online world means that the quantity of resources available to students now is massive: so much choice is available that making a plan has got harder, not easier.

- **What counts as enough?** Making a plan involves boundaries and deciding when to stop. This can get harder and harder for students as they get older and move into course content where it just isn't possible to finish everything.

It's time to explore how we can help students understand the nuances of agency, and how we can support them in being more confident about making a plan.

Key takeaways

- Students who believe in their ability to make and stick to a revision plan are less likely to experience problematic levels of exam stress.
- When students believe that they are able to achieve an outcome, there is inevitably the risk that they blame themselves if they are not successful.
- Many students find it difficult to make a realistic revision plan.

Questions for reflection

- When students are disappointed with their results, do they blame themselves or do they have a balanced understanding of which bits they are responsible for and which factors lie beyond their control?
- What do your students find difficult about planning their revision?

You can do anything if you want it enough – is this true?

We had one English teacher – we all thought she was really strict but she was better at helping us manage our stress. She gave me advice – she told me to control the controllables. I still remember this now.

University student

A few years ago I worked at an academically selective independent school. One year I was part of the team doing the general interviews for admission. We often used 'Tell me about a book you are reading' as the opening question. I remember one girl whose face suddenly brightened when I asked her this. 'I've been reading *Becoming* by Michelle Obama,' she said. 'It has inspired me because it has made me realise that I can make my dreams come true if I really want to.'

I'm ashamed to admit that I was more irritated by this than I probably should have been. Maybe it was because it was the 15th interview of the morning and I was fading; maybe it was because the answer had the strong whiff of pre-prepared-by-her family and learned-off-by-heart. The girl was 10 years old; I was a bit sceptical about whether she had actually read the book. 'Do you *really* believe that?' I asked. 'Yes,' she said. 'Michelle Obama says so.'

I didn't challenge her any further: it wouldn't have been fair. *You can do anything* has become so embedded a notion in popular culture that it doesn't really encourage scepticism. Take any reality TV programme you like where people get to succeed, and then play *you can do anything* bingo. Wait and see how long it takes for someone to say this and for the collective cheer of agreement to reverberate.

The notion is not entirely without truth: hard work, determination, commitment – these are all things that can overtake the natural advantages of talent and opportunity. Malcolm Gladwell's book *Outliers: The Story of Success* established the now popular idea of 10,000 hours (Gladwell, 2009). Practice, Gladwell argues, is the essence of success: practise anything for 10,000 hours and you'll reach top-level attainment.

The problem with the *you can do anything, it just takes hard work* ethos is that it does not account for luck or the limited nature of time. When students are preparing for exams, the timeline is fixed: they need to be realistic about what is possible in the finite number of hours available. In addition, no matter how effective their revision is, there's always the risk of an unforeseen externality: maybe an entirely unexpected question comes up, maybe their teacher was absent for a crucial lesson and the cover work didn't really do it justice, maybe their exam marker has a brain-scrunching headache and can't concentrate. We need to recognise that *make a plan* is a good way to improve things, but it doesn't take away the risk altogether. We need to be honest with teenagers that – even clutching their revision plan – it would be natural to feel some degree of worry all the same. The outcome for public exams is never guaranteed in advance.

I often tell my students that when I stack up all my job applications, the unsuccessful pile is the bigger one. I say this to them because I want them to know that sometimes it works out, sometimes it doesn't, and the variables in the situation may have nothing to do with individual agency at all. It's understandable to want to believe that they can make their dreams come true if they want it enough, that there's a guaranteed route-map to success if only they can unlock enough motivation and self-belief. The hard reality is that it's just not as simple as that. Making a plan is a very good idea, for sure, but we need to be clear that it's not a silver bullet: it improves our chances but it does not guarantee everything.

Key takeaways

- *You can do anything if you want it enough*: this is not entirely true.
- Students need realistic goals.
- Students have to learn to live with uncertain outcomes; there are always external factors beyond their control.
- Making a plan will help students succeed and it will help them feel that preparation is more manageable, but it won't stop all the pre-exam nerves.

Questions for reflection

- How often do you think your students hear the message that they can do anything if they try hard enough?
- How does your school help families understand what realistic targets look like?
- How often do students get to discuss the idea of external factors beyond their control?
- Does your school help its students understand that pre-exam nerves are inevitable to some degree and that working harder won't stop the nerves altogether?

Responsibility and self-blame: *Just do your best* – is this helpful?

My stress probably started in Year 10 – it started to get real. The main pressure was because in Year 9 we did ability tests – verbal reasoning, intelligence tests. I got highlighted in my year group as someone who could get 7 A*s or more. The headteacher contacted my parents – they were really happy. At the time,

The problem with the *you can do anything* catch phrase isn't only that it's a bit of an illusion. The other problem rests in the agency-responsibility-self-blame nexus. As Chapter 3 will explain, one of the characteristics of our brain is an inclination for coherence: our thought processes join the dots between similar situations and ideas, creating a simplified, coherent picture that connects them all. We need to recognise that – for teenagers navigating the run-up to GCSEs – the *you can do anything* messaging can shift seamlessly into something much less encouraging: *by the way*, says the mirror-image whisper, *the only obstacle to success is you.*

Much of the analysis in Chapter 1 explored the well-intentioned but often unhelpful standard response of *you don't need to worry*. Equally common and equally well intentioned is to offer reassurance by the easy tag line, *just do your best.*

I used to say it all the time. I can remember handing out end-of-year exam papers: *thwunk* was the sound as the paper hit the student's desk; *just do your best* was my cheerful reassurance. I also remember one of the first times I really listened to a student who had broken down because her stress was overwhelming. I asked her where her worry about outcomes came from. 'Do your parents want you to get a particular grade?' I asked. 'Oh no,' she said, 'it's not that; all they want is for me to do my best.' The problem she faced was that this left her feeling like – however hard she tried – if there was more she could have done, then she hadn't tried hard enough.

Sometimes we need to pause and hear the words that we say. *Just do your best* is easy to say, but it's also an instruction that is almost impossible for anyone to fulfil. Our optimal long-term performance mode is necessarily some way short of our actual short-term best: if I run a marathon, it's necessary to run much more slowly than in a 100m sprint. As Chapter 4 will explore in more detail, teenagers find it hard to balance short-term decisions with a long-term perspective. Going to bed, taking a break, choosing not to do that little bit more: to the teenage mind, does that count as really doing their best?

Just do your reasonable best in these circumstances. Just do the amount that can be sustained in the long term, without shutting off other parts of your life. That would be a better, more nuanced message. But it also brings its own challenges: what does *reasonable* actually look like? How is a teenager supposed to be confident that their decisions about what to do and when to stop aren't going to sell themselves short and leave them open to criticism and feelings of failure? The *Strategies to use* later in this chapter will offer ideas about how to support students in these types of decisions.

In my context – it's a girls' selective school – some put a lot of pressure on themselves, either through their own high standards or sometimes from home as well. Some of them want to get full marks all the time.

Academic Lead for Y11

Key takeaways

- Agency involves responsibility and responsibility can bring guilt and self-blame.
- *Just do your best* is advice that is impossible to fulfil; it can make it hard for the most motivated students to feel that they've done enough.
- We need to help students work out what their reasonable best looks like.

Making choices

> *Pupils get overwhelmed because they can't prioritise: it's too much to contemplate and so they can't do any of it. The fear of starting can be big: students are worried that if they're not performing to where they want to be or where other people expect them to be, then someone will judge that. Sometimes they get a bit stuck in thinking that they have to be a certain way or get a certain grade. This can be harder for kids with SEND – it's harder to think flexibly about different outcomes.*
>
> 11–18 SENDCO

Making choices about revision is genuinely difficult; it involves questions that do not have easy answers. For example:

- **How long should I work for?** One hour extra per night? 1.25 hours? 1.5? Push it to 2? There is no easy answer to that question. What one student achieves in 30 minutes might take someone else 1.5 hours to complete; one student might have the physical stamina to concentrate until 10pm but another might not. Some students revise by watching videos in a low-intensity way; some students work in a way that is so focused it can't be sustained for over long periods of time. Teenagers often try to use their friends as a metric for what they should do, but when it comes to revision, comparison with others is only so helpful.

- **Which work should I prioritise?** If students are lucky, they will have teachers who help them with this, but it takes a very confident teacher to say to a class that one part of the syllabus matters more than another. I remember hearing another teacher at a Year 11 parents' evening giving advice about what to prioritise. *Of course,* she said, *don't de-prioritise the other bits.* Prioritising involves not doing something else; that's the hard bit of the decision and it's the bit teachers and students often shy away from.

- **Which resources should I use?** When it came to revision, my generation had their textbook, class notes and perhaps a few practice questions if their teacher was particularly industrious. But for today's students, available online will be lesson slides, links to multiple revision websites such as BBC Bitesize, online learning tools and additional lesson resources from online learning platforms. Then there are past papers, mark schemes, sample answers, examiners' comments. Then there are published revision guides, often more than one to choose from for any particular subject.

All of this means that the most likely scenario is that students are told to make a plan, they are told all the different things that they could be doing in their revision, but the actual decision about what to focus on and when falls to them. Teenagers need to make their own decisions, that's part of growing up: if we took away all opportunities for them to find their own agency, we would do them no favours at all. But at the same time, it's important to recognise why this decision-making has become so difficult.

This decision-making is difficult right across the attainment range. For students whose grades are low, the scale of the to-do list can make them feel like there's no point doing anything at all – *what's the point? It's not going to make any difference anyway.* For students who are pushing for the top grades, it's hard to know when to stop. The *Strategies to use* section at the end of this chapter will offer some ideas about how we can support students in their revision decisions.

> *I've had two bottom-set Year 11 classes: the level of disengagement has been frightening in a few of them, especially if they have missed learning in school for a variety of reasons. This sense of* I can't *drowns the other voices that are encouraging and telling them that they can do it. I think what adds to this stress is that they know they've missed so much learning along the way – then they think* what's the point in trying now? It's far too daunting. It's easier just to give up.*
>
> Assistant Head – Teaching and Learning

> *I feel like it's hard to feel like you've done enough. For chemistry, for example, if you finish all the questions in the revision packs – maybe then I'd feel I'd done enough, but I probably wouldn't stop. You feel like there's always more to do – there are so many legacy papers.*
>
> Year 13 student

Key takeaways

- Making a revision plan involves deciding how long to work for, which work to do and which resources to use.
- Online resources have made these decisions more complicated.
- Deciding what not to prioritise can be really difficult.

Questions for reflection

- Do you give options for different revision resources or do you encourage students to limit what they use?
- How do your students work out which revision resources to use, which content to prioritise and when to stop?

The long-term trajectory for hyper-engaged students: a perfect plan or revising enough?

The difficulties of making a plan can overwhelm and de-motivate students at any level, but there is an additional risk factor for the conscientious students whose commitment and drive could end up tipping into damaging hyper-engagement. The more hard-working a student is, the easier it is to duck out of the difficult responsibility that prioritisation brings. At Key Stage 3 or GCSE, the hard-working student can simply plan to do everything.

The big problem, however, is that this then sets an unrealistic expectation for future exams. Syllabuses are bigger for A levels and bigger again at degree level. The need to make choices about what to prioritise becomes more and more important. As Chapter 4 will discuss, GCSEs take place at a very formative time in the brain's development. Dispositions embedded at that time can be hard to shake off. Exam stress can build over time as it becomes harder and harder for students to achieve the reassuring sense of completion that was possible in their first – and arguably most formative – set of public exams.

> I've got students who have gone to Oxford or Cambridge, but some of those bright kids put far more pressure on themselves than some of their peers. They are more conscious of what they're lacking but also how much is at stake that they do well. One of my students is now at Oxford but she put so much pressure on herself that she froze in one of her exam papers – she was shaking, crying.
>
> Assistant Head – Teaching and Learning

Just do your best: the simplicity of this message isn't only because it is four words long. It's also because the maximum of anything is a much simpler cut-off point than the much looser idea of enough. *Just do your reasonable best, do enough, not everything*: as students move forward and progress into increasingly demanding terrain, *enough* becomes harder and harder to pin down. As the student below describes, ambition can end up driving a young person into a position where, because there is always somewhere further to go, whatever they achieve is – put simply – never enough for them to feel like they can stop.

> When the academic anxiety began at A level, it felt good to be good at school work. I was top of the class in most of my classes. This made me feel good, but there was always a sense of unrest – if I got 39/40, then I felt that I should get 40/40. I'd always focus on the mistakes. I was always doing more work than other people and it got to the point where it became unhealthy. Now I find myself obsessing about everything I do, if it's not perfect then it's terrible. It felt like a constant weight on my shoulders, always the sense that it could be better, it could be better.
>
> University student

There is a considerable overlap between natural ambition and the risk that this ambition tips into an unhealthily demanding set of self-imposed standards. Perfectionism can become a debilitating mindset, resulting in self-criticism, lowered self-esteem and impaired performance. It is also often associated with mental-health problems such as anxiety, depression and eating difficulties. As the authors of *Overcoming Perfectionism* (Sharfran et al., 2018 pp.13–14) state, 'there is no clear-cut distinction between positive and negative striving to meet standards. Often, setting demanding standards can start out as positive but over time become negative… Someone can have the goal of completing all their reading lists at school, and that is appropriate; but in a different context, such as at university, it is just not realistic to expect to read everything.'

Key takeaways

- Making a plan and getting it all done feels comforting and rewarding, but this gets harder to achieve as students move to more advanced courses.
- Getting everything done can tip into perfectionism.
- Deciding what counts as enough is difficult, especially when it involves deliberately leaving things out.

Questions for reflection

- Do you encourage your students to identify their priorities and decide what to leave out if they are short of time?
- Does the idea of helping students decide what to leave out make you uneasy? What does this show you about how the students might be feeling?

Strategies to use #1: A nuanced approach to messaging

Whole-school messaging can be very difficult to get right: some really do need to work harder but some really need to be told to take their foot off the gas. There's the year-assembly conundrum: do you say to the whole group, well done, this has gone really well or do you say, you need to work on these things – how do you set the tone?

Senior Deputy Head

There is no doubt that whole-group messaging feels tricky: the year-assembly conundrum above applies just as much to an individual class. Some students need to work harder, some students need to ease off a bit. When it comes to how much work to do, there simply isn't a one-size-fits-all answer.

The key idea in this chapter, however, is that we need to be wary of simple sound bites which end up distorting the picture. Effective year-group messaging doesn't rest on finding a single instruction that suits everyone; it rests on helping students understand better the realities – and complexities – of the relationship between their efforts and the grade outcome. In the table below, you can see the difference between the simple sound bite and the more nuanced, truthful statement.

The following table is also available as an online resource for download at bloomsbury.pub/exam-stress.

Simple sound bite	More nuanced statement
Just do your best.	*You need to strike a balance between working hard enough to fulfil your goals and working so hard that you impact your overall wellbeing.*
If you've worked hard enough, you've got nothing to worry about.	*Working hard will help you achieve your goals, but don't be surprised if you still feel worried about how the test will go. This is natural because there is always a degree of uncertainty. If you're feeling stressed about how much there is to do, don't underestimate the value of doing just something: you don't have to do everything.*
If you want it enough, you can make your dreams come true.	*To achieve your goals, you need perseverance: sometimes things go well, and sometimes they don't. That's life: there's always a degree of chance. Sometimes, outcomes are driven by things you can't control.*
You need to make a revision plan.	*Making a revision plan is important, but it can involve difficult decisions about what to work on, which resources to use and how long to spend on it. We'll be spending time thinking about this so you can be confident your choices are sensible.*

Strategies to use #2: Tolerating the uncertainty of an outcome

As a child and adolescent psychotherapist I see the teenagers who are struggling the most with their anxiety. These pupils are terrified. They are living in fear. I'm thinking of two Year 13s. They can't eat. They are making themselves ill. They are studying constantly. They are living off fear. They are so full of what-ifs – what if my mind goes blank, what if this one thing comes up that I don't know? *It's really helpful to be able to talk through possible outcomes. I did an exercise today with a young person talking through the what-ifs; it was all survivable but teenagers need help to get to a place where they know that it is survivable.*

Child and adolescent psychotherapist

At the core of the unease about revision, agency, responsibility and choices is the inevitable degree of uncertainty about outcome. A key part of supportive messaging involves helping students see beyond the outcome to the positive next step that could come next.

When students are worried about getting lower grades than they're aiming for, the prospect can be so uncomfortable that they do not engage with thinking about *what then…?* I've met with many parents who were worried that their children were about to 'fail' their GCSEs. I used to say to them *OK, we need to think about how to improve things, but you also need to look at that worst-case scenario head on – and you need to talk to your child about positive next steps if it happens.*

Missing the grades for sixth form college or university can be a big disappointment, but it's not the end of everything: helping students to see the up-sides of Plan B will help them feel calmer about the risk that their revision choices might not generate the outcome they want the most.

Equally important is to help students see what they get to take from the process that is valuable, regardless of outcome. The table below distinguishes between an all-or-nothing mindset, which can't tolerate the risk of it all going wrong, and a more balanced mindset, which sees value either way.

The following table and questions are also available as an online resource for download at bloomsbury.pub/exam-stress.

All-or-nothing mindset	Balanced mindset
I've got to get my grades because I can't go to Newcastle University if I don't.	*I really want to go to Newcastle University, and I'll be very disappointed if I don't. It will take me time to adjust to the prospect of going somewhere else, but I know that there'll be an upside. I've been checking out the website for Liverpool again, and x, y, z looks really good.*
If I don't get my grades, all this revision will have been a total waste of time.	*It'll be really disappointing to miss my grades after all this hard work, but I know that I've learned useful skills about how to pace myself and structure my time. These will be useful to me in the future.*

As teachers, we can help our students develop a value-either-way mindset by asking them questions such as:

- *What do you think you'll do if you don't get the grades? What are the upsides of this outcome?*
- *What skills do you think you're developing at the moment? How will these skills help you in the future?*
- *Imagine this work isn't going to be assessed: what value are you getting from it that isn't to do with the grade outcome?*

Strategies to use #3: The framework for revision

Students do need to make their own revision plans; if we did this for them, they wouldn't get the opportunity to practise and get better at the difficult decision-making involved. What we can do, though, is ask the questions that help students plan and sense-check their decisions, so that our students feel more confident that their plan is a good one.

You can create the space for intentional thinking about revision by asking questions like those below.

A worksheet based on the following questions is available as an online resource for download at bloomsbury.pub/exam-stress.

- *How much time can you realistically allocate to this revision?* Students often over-estimate how much work they will do; it's important to help them be realistic about how little time may be available. If students are struggling to come up with a number, then an imaginary example can help, factoring in the number of days available and a realistic distribution of time across those days for the different subjects.
- *Let's imagine you have three blocks of one hour available for revision: you may not be able to cover everything. What are your priorities, and why? What are you not going to do?*
- *What revision materials are you going to use and why? Which materials are you not going to use and why?*
- *What are you going to do with those revision materials? What are you not going to do?*

Giving 10–15 minutes of lesson time to these types of questions creates the opportunity for students to write down and review their answers. This will help to make sure that students have the space to think about revision in a structured, realistic way. Hearing a teacher say *that sounds like a good idea* can be transformative in helping build confidence; hearing a teacher legitimise the idea that not everything is equally important can help students feel less overwhelmed by the potential size of the revision-guide to-do list.

It's always tempting as a teacher to lead from the front and give a sweeping overview of all the different things that a student could do when revising. Flipping this round and asking students to verbalise and explain what they are – and are not – going to do has two major benefits: it makes sure students practise planning their decisions and it means there's room for constructive advice if the planning decisions are clearly going awry.

Learning to understand the nuances of responsibility and decision-making takes time, thought, maturity and insight; as Chapter 4 will discuss, all of these are things that are still evolving in the adolescent brain. Moving from simple concepts to a mature understanding of complexity and nuance is at the core of human development; I would argue that it's one of the driving aims of education. But it's difficult: simple concepts are easier and, as it turns out, the fastest, busiest bits of our mental processing capacities thrive on them. To understand why, we need now to step into the footsteps of cognitive scientists. It's time for Chapter 3.

Areas for action

- If a student seems stressed about revising for an exam, help them to be realistic about the time available and how much can be done in this time; role-model calm, pragmatic thinking, focused on achievable goals.
- Make sure that you help students practise prioritising; this includes verbalising what they are not going to do and why.
- If you think a student is working too hard, raise this as a concern with the pastoral team. Addressing hyper-engagement at an early stage reduces the risk that it embeds as perfectionism, driving targets which become increasingly difficult to meet over time.

3 How we think

Pupils always hear more deeply the bits that correlate with what they already believe to be true.

Senior Deputy Head

Starting points

Why do we keep thinking in simple maxims such as *you can do anything*? Why is it so difficult for an adolescent to keep in mind the conflicting nuances within a concept? Why is it tricky for a student to remember at one and the same time that they are responsible for getting their grades but it is not always their fault if things don't work out? This chapter will focus on why we think in the way that we do, drawing on Daniel Kahneman's groundbreaking research into the patterns and biases that keep pulling us towards simplified thought patterns.

Thought processes: System 1 and System 2

In the 1980s, psychologists Daniel Kahneman and Amos Tversky published a paper that fundamentally changed understanding of how we think: their focus was on the biases that occur when we are thinking quickly.

Their 1980s paper was the first step on the way to years of research that focused in part on why we keep making use of simple concepts rather than their more accurate, nuanced versions. Their research laid the foundations for behavioural economics and in 2002 their work was awarded a Nobel Prize. In 2012 Kahneman published a summary of their findings: *Thinking, Fast and Slow*. If you are looking for a book that really will change your understanding of how we think, it's one to read. What's more, its conclusions are directly relevant to an understanding of why unease about grade outcomes can become so embedded in a teenager's mind.

Kahneman's analysis divides our thought processes into two systems, System 1 and System 2. System 1 and System 2 don't refer to separate areas of the brain in the way that neuroscientific labels do, but they offer a convenient way for us to understand the differences between our careful, conscious, slow thinking and the involuntary, intuitive, quick responses that get thrown up by brain processes that operate invisibly behind the scenes.

System 1 is fast and involuntary. It is the thought process that gives us seemingly instant answers: if someone asks you the answer to 2+2, System 1 will give you the answer 4. System 1 works quickly and automatically: you had no choice about whether or not to think about the answer; it was there before you could do anything about it. Some of System 1's capacities are innate, such as its ability to recognise emotion; other capacities are developed through practice, such as basic multiplication, reading or technical skills in sport, music or similar. If we tried to map System 1 onto areas in the brain, its functionality would include aspects of the rational as well as the emotional regions.

System 2 is slow and deliberate. It deals with the situations where System 1 falls short. If we are asked the answer to 27×39, we probably need to sit down and work it out carefully, using System 2. System 2 is slow and laborious, and we get a choice about whether or not to engage it. If we are aware that we are thinking something through, that's System 2 in operation.

Kahneman argues that slow-thinking System 2 is not our default mode. Most of the time we make use of the output from fast-thinking System 1, a system that is always active, invisibly giving us the information that shapes our responses. As Kahneman writes, 'most impressions and thoughts arise in your conscious experience without your knowing how they got there' (Kahneman, 2012, p.4). In addition, even when we do engage System 2, much of the input it uses comes from System 1. If we upset someone, we might use System 2 to work out how to make things better, but our awareness that the other person was upset in the first place, our involuntary feelings of unease or guilt, our unquestioning belief that 2am is not the best time to phone them up – all of that is probably the result of System 1.

This means that our thought patterns are dominated by System 1. Kahneman's research explores the ways that fast-thinking System 1 shapes the thoughts it produces. This chapter will focus on why this is relevant to an understanding of exam stress. The following sections will focus on three key factors that influence our System 1 thoughts, exploring how and why they give rise to stress about exams.

- **Priming:** System 1 thoughts are impacted by previous experiences.
- **Simplicity:** System 1 thrives on quick, simple concepts.
- **Coherence**: System 1 is more likely to focus on material that confirms previous experience.

Key takeaways

- Some of our thoughts arise in our brains instantly and in a way that we do not get to control: these thoughts are from fast-thinking System 1.
- Some of our System 1 thoughts arise from innate abilities, such as recognising emotions in others.
- Some of our System 1 thoughts result from skills and knowledge that have been practised so much they have become automatic, such as reading or basic maths.
- If we are aware that we are thinking something through, we are using System 2.
- Most of our thoughts come from System 1.

Questions for reflection

- What sorts of things in your day-to-day life can you do without really thinking about it? If you are making a cup of tea, are you really thinking about what you are doing?
- What sorts of things do you say in the classroom by habit rather than by deliberate choice?
- Can you think of examples where you have felt your own reluctance to use System 2 – maybe writing a difficult email, completing a job application or planning a lesson you have never taught before?

Priming

Not everyone fears the same event to the same degree. One of the contributing factors for this is the subjective colouring created by our different previous experiences.

One of the reasons we are able to make so many decisions so quickly – and successfully – is because of System 1's ability to retrieve information about relevant previous experience and use this to help us understand what to do next. As Kahneman exemplifies, System 1 allows us to recognise that if someone raises their hand in a restaurant, they're probably asking for the bill; if someone raises their hand while looking into the road in central London, they're probably hailing a taxi; but if someone raises their hand when they approach someone in a dark alley, it's probably not good news. We'll respond accordingly, probably without pausing to think about what we are doing.

System 1 works invisibly: we are not aware of which memories it is using and how. This means that sometimes our responses are influenced by factors in a way we would never have realised, and this is where priming comes in. Kahneman's research was based around experiments designed to reveal how exposure to one thing impacts the associations that something else evokes, even if they appear unrelated. For example, one of his experiments demonstrated that if someone is shown the word 'eat' and then the word 'so-p', they are much more likely to read 'so-p' as 'soup' than as 'soap', but if someone else is shown the word 'wash' then the reverse happens. A different experiment tracked contributions to an honesty box for use of tea and coffee facilities in a university staff kitchen. Over a period of 10 weeks, different pictures were put up on the wall above the honesty box. Each picture stayed up for a week at a time and the content of the pictures alternated between watchful eyes and pretty flowers. In each of the weeks where the watchful eyes were displayed on the wall, contributions to the honesty box were markedly higher (Kahneman, 2012).

Thinking about factors that prime a student's reaction

In the context of exam stress, priming means that a student's response to a test is shaped by multiple factors, some of which they will be aware of and some of which they won't. If a teacher tells the class at the start of the test that the results really matter, it will be fairly obvious to the students that this might impact how they feel about the outcomes. But if they heard their parents at the weekend congratulating their neighbour for great GCSE results, it's entirely possible that their response to the test will have been primed by this experience, whether or not they realise it.

Students sometimes find it difficult to explain why they feel so anxious about exam outcomes. This is no surprise: much of the causal chain behind their response takes place invisibly, in the seemingly instantaneous processing of System 1. Learning to understand their reactions, therefore, requires seeing links that their brains created for them in a way which bypassed their conscious awareness.

> *Pupils find it hard to articulate why they feel the pressure that they do. They find it hard to see a connection with what their parents, peer group or teachers are saying: they don't correlate their feelings with, e.g., the fact that they heard a friend saying they've revised five hours a day for a test – they don't see the connection between this and the fact they are now feeling stressed about the same test. They don't correlate the pressure they put on themselves with the fact that they've heard their parents talking about their Oxbridge degrees and how that has shaped their sense of how important academic outcomes are.*
>
> 11–18 Deputy Head Pastoral

If we want to understand why some students are so worried, we need to think searchingly about the external factors that prime someone's response. We need to think about the messages that they receive when they are not in the exam room, as well as the experiences they have when they are sitting that exam. As Chapter 5 will explore, we need to understand the range of input used by System 1 to generate the unhelpful, inaccurate and problematic response that *yes, you may say this is only a test, but actually, this situation warrants fear.*

In addition, as the *Strategies to use* section at the end of this chapter will explore, we need to think about how to help our students recognise when their System 1 thought processes throw up a response that is – in some way – inaccurate or unhelpful.

The need for simplicity

Blunt categorisation

System 1's most important characteristic is that it is fast: it throws up answers pretty much instantly. It should be no surprise, therefore, to hear that Kahneman's research demonstrates that System 1 likes simplicity. Simplicity makes decision-making easier and quicker, but it also means that System 1 has to operate on fairly blunt, simplified categorisations.

Our survival-focused mental hardwiring means that we need System 1 to be able to notice a wild animal charging at us, put it in the category of *things that run quickly towards us can be dangerous* and initiate our fight or flight response. Crucially, we need it to be able to do this at lightning speed, and probably before we've even had the chance to notice consciously what it is that is moving at pace towards us in the distance. The blunt categorisation, however, will also mean that we're likely to flinch in the cinema when an animal charges suddenly on screen – especially if it's 3D – or if a friend jokingly takes a pretend swipe at us, even if we know – rationally – that there is no threat there at all.

Blunt categorisations have a significant impact on how students think about assessments. System 1's readiness to simplify means that rather than holding onto the complex thought that *I can do this bit, but not that bit, and if I put 20 minutes into learning these five things I'll add 10% and so it's worth putting that bit of effort in*, it's much easier to think *I don't know anything, I'm just gonna fail*. The same thing can happen for the high-achievers: *this bit of the syllabus is difficult, I'm not totally on top of it but the likely mark differential is probably only 3% so it's not worth fixating on*. This is a complex, evaluative thought: it's much quicker, easier and simpler to think *I've got to get this bit right or I'm going to do badly in the whole exam*.

The areas where I came across exam stress the most were as a form tutor. The one student I dealt with most as a tutor got nearly all 9s. On the face of it she had absolutely zero need to be concerned about anything. The first time she came to me she was worried she was going to fail her history – this was after her mock – she thought she'd done terribly, but in fact she got a 9 in this paper.

Early career teacher

In addition, if a student is mildly worried about their French oral mock, fairly confident about the biology paper but really worried about the English literature essay questions, it's easier for System 1 to use a much simpler concept and throw up the thought *I'm worried about the mocks in general*. To make matters worse for the anxious student, the brain's readiness to think in blunt categorisations is exacerbated by anxiety: cognitive behavioural therapy often focuses on the cognitive distortions that anxiety can produce, such as catastrophising, overgeneralising and black-and-white thinking (Haidt, 2024).

I definitely catastrophise, I definitely feel that if I make a mistake then I've failed the whole thing. If you do one paper and you skip a question, it's natural to ponder on that for a long time. 100% you catastrophise about how it's gone. Also you can't determine whether the question was hard or whether you didn't apply yourself enough. I know loads of people feel this way.

Year 13 student

The simplification of like/dislike

There's a further consequence of System 1's need for speed and simplicity: if it is faced with a question that it can't answer easily, it is very likely to swap it for an easier one instead. For example, if I'm asked whether I like one political party's educational policies better than another political party's and I'm feeling a bit hazy over the details of each, there's a very good chance that my System 1 will substitute an easier question and consider instead which political party I like more in general. If I don't pause and deliberately engage System 2 in order to question my knee-jerk response, it's very likely that System 1 will impel me to offer up its first answer, even though it's the result of a simplified thought process driven by the very basic like/dislike metric.

This means that the simple metric of like/dislike plays a significant role in our responses, and probably more than we realise (Kahneman, 2012). This adds another dimension to our understanding of exam stress: uncomfortable feelings that are difficult to understand or verbalise are likely to get simplified into *I just don't like it*. We all know how often students write a subject off – *I hate Maths, English is pointless, why do we have to read this useless poem?* Nervousness about doing badly easily warps into the simple response of *I don't want to do it at all*, exacerbating the downwards spiral of disengagement that often takes place.

> *After the exams you end up thinking about it – if it had gone well, that motivated me to work for the others. If it feels like it's gone badly, then it's harder to revise for the others.*
>
> Year 12 student

> *In our context there's also a bit of* our school is rubbish, everyone does rubbish, so what's the point? *We've had the Ofsted ranking to contend with – we're in special measures. We have a lot of disengagement – if you give students an assessment, they don't do very well, then they say* I can't do it, why bother? *They say* I can't do science, science is really hard. *I've had multiple parents saying* science is hard, I couldn't do it. *If they're getting this message from home, that's an additional challenge for us.*
>
> Physics teacher

Questions for reflection

- Think about the way students talk about assessments: do you hear them talk in specifics or in blunt generalisations?
- How often do you see like/dislike override a student's ability to be more evaluative about how well something will go or the likely benefits of doing something?

Coherence and categorisation

Confirmation bias

Kahneman's research tells us that the trump card in System 1's rapid-fire skill set is associative memory: this brain function allows us to integrate sets of information. Associative memory knits together separate experiences, likening them to each other, establishing categories and creating a coherent picture of what that category of experience is all about (Kahneman, 2012). What this means is that System 1 is superb at recognising similarities: *this is like that, and therefore I can use my knowledge about that to help me work out what to do with this.*

Unfortunately, this means that there is a major confirmation bias built into our quick-fire responses. System 1's need for coherence means that once we decide that, for example, someone does not like us, we are much more likely to notice details which confirm this interpretation. In the context of exam stress, this means that once a child has the impression that they are 'bad' at science, they will notice their mistakes much more readily than the things that go well. *My teacher never asks me when I've got my hand up, I never understand anything, the lessons are always so boring*: think how often students speak about situations as if they are always exactly the same.

For the student who believes they are worried about school assessments, once this idea is in their mind, it is much more likely that their System 1 processes their experiences in a way that confirms rather than overrides their worries about the exam.

Pupil self-perception can be kick-started by the tiniest of messaging, e.g. around their results in a Year 7 maths test. If this leaves them thinking they are bad at maths, then it only takes a couple more comments for this to start to snowball into thinking that this is their identity.

Head of Y9

Categorisation and simplification

Kahneman's research demonstrates that we are able to think so quickly because we use prior experience to help us understand present situations. This process depends on our ability to create categories within our experience. For example, if I walk into a building I've never been in before, my ability to categorise is what allows me to recognise it as a church or a museum and behave in a different way from the way I'd behave in a café or shop.

If we pause, however, to consider the process of categorisation, we can see how difficult it is to do. I remember when my children were young and in the *what's that* phase of language development: *what's that there?* I'd start out confidently: *that's a car, that's a train, that's a bus*. But the problem is that neat categories don't really exist in the way they do in the picture books. How about the small people-carrier that looks a bit like a van? When does a bus become a coach? Is a roofed motorbike a car or a bike? Categorisation requires us to ignore the fine-grained detail of the differences between situations; it encourages us to focus instead on similarities.

Chapter 2 explored the idea of mirror-image whispers and our readiness to hear one thing but simultaneously absorb its mirror-image counterpart: *you can do anything if you want it enough* can become blurred with *it's your fault if it doesn't work out*. System 1's love of coherence is the engine room behind this: *you can do it if you try hard enough* and *it's all your fault if you don't succeed* are ideas that are related, but they are not exactly the same thing. *You can do it if you try hard enough* says that effort generates outcomes. *It's all your fault if you don't succeed* claims that the only causal factor for an outcome is effort. System 1 merrily simplifies, ignores the fine-grained differences and equates both to the same basic concept that *outcome depends on effort; if it goes wrong, it's your fault*.

False expectations

The brain's need for coherence also means that we carry forward dispositions embedded by previous experiences. Often these are useful but not always. For the student, their experience of secondary school is shaped by things that happened at primary school; the A level student has a perception that is coloured by GCSE messaging; the university student will instinctively expect more of the same at university. In Part 2, this book will explore how one phase of study impacts another, how messaging received years earlier can create false expectations about a later situation, even if it is fundamentally different in nature. It will also explore how the brain's readiness to default to System 1 means that rewriting expectations often requires really deliberate, intentional System 2 thinking. The *Strategies to use* section at the end of this chapter offers some ideas about how to help students practise this intentional System 2 thinking to correct the biases of System 1.

> *The move from A level to university was a much bigger change than GCSE to A level. You can't just make flashcards for everything you study. Adapting the study methods to something much more fast-paced was really difficult: the amount you're taught and expected to know is insane in comparison to A level, but what you actually need for the exam isn't so much: I found it difficult to accept that you're not going to know everything.*
>
> University student

Key takeaways

- Associative memory allows us to link experiences together into categories.
- Fast-thinking System 1 has an in-built confirmation bias: it's likely to interpret a situation in a way that fits with previous experience and beliefs.

(cont.)

> **Questions for reflection**
>
> - Have you seen confirmation bias at work in the way students talk about their school experiences? If they decide they don't like something, is there a tendency only to notice when it goes badly?
> - Think about how often students expect to do things in the same way as they did before: do you hear students say things like *but last year we did …?*

Why students need to know about System 1 and System 2

A stressful situation: is it a challenge or a threat? This is a central question for exam-stress analysis. A challenge is great, it's an opportunity for success; a threat kick-starts the fear-response. For the student trying to get their head around how well something might go, it's a complicated sum: *this bit might be OK; this bit might not be, but this section is worth more than that section and maybe that question won't come up.* This sort of complex evaluation is not fast-thinking System 1's forte: the student needs to engage slow-thinking System 2.

> *Stepping away from your work, calming yourself down – this helps: saying to yourself to take it steady, go over your work, don't speed everything. Then go back to it.*
>
> Year 12 student

Unfortunately, engaging System 2 is not the default. As Kahneman demonstrates, the brain likes efficiency and System 2 takes effort. If we can manage without it, we do. System 2 is hard work. There's only so much bandwidth in the brain and if we have to engage System 2, it limits our ability to multi-task. Kahneman offers a useful example of this: if you are going for a walk with a friend, it's easy enough to chat as you walk. But if the friend asks you a difficult question – 23×52, for example – you'll probably stop walking in order to think about it (Kahneman, 2012). This is one of the reasons why knowledge-fluency underpins popular teaching methodologies such as Rosenshine's ten principles (Rosenshine, 2010; Sherrington, 2019). When knowledge retrieval is quick and easy, it sits in the domain of System 1; this frees up System 2 to think about it. System 2 can only do so much at once: if System 2 is needed for remembering, there won't be much space for thinking at all.

The bandwidth model also explains why it can be so difficult for an anxious student to remodel their relationship with schoolwork. The physical consequences of stress are gruelling enough on their own: it's hard to sleep, it can be difficult to eat, it's a strain to concentrate properly. Pausing to engage System 2 to think very methodically through the likely success/failure prospects requires mental energy that the student probably feels they do not have. It's no surprise that – in the midst of exam nerves – the most likely thing a student will say is *I don't want to talk about it*. In the absence of bringing System 2 into the mix, System's 1 blunt, simple, fast generalisations rule supreme.

It feels like everything is going fast – like the exams are coming – it's faster and faster, you don't have that time to revise. It makes it harder to work – it makes me panic – my brain just goes blank.

Year 12 student

If we want to help reduce exam nerves, we need to help students understand the mechanics of System 1 so that they can learn to moderate its conclusions with the more nuanced capabilities of System 2. Crucially, we need to do it at an early stage, before the consequences of anxiety take up so much bandwidth that it becomes nearly impossible for the student to bring System 2 into the mix. We can do this by adopting the three following strategies.

Strategies to use #1: Teaching the difference between System 1 and System 2

Before I read Kahneman's book, I had never thought about where my quick-fire thoughts came from. That's no surprise: the key characteristic of System 1 is that we don't notice it in action. How does anyone learn to think about something they have never noticed?

Once you start noticing it, however, it's easy to see how it's there all the time. As teachers, if we comment on it, we can help students to become self-aware. The list below contains examples of how we can do this in the classroom.

- *We're going to do some quick-fire questions and answers: I'm looking for System 1 responses – don't pause to think!*
- *Let's remember that our System 1 thought processes create simple, generalised conclusions: 'Macbeth is a coward' – is that a System 1 answer or System 2 response?*
- *You've just said that your chemistry teacher always finishes late: has your System 1 generalised here? Is what you've said actually always true?*
- *What do you mean you don't want to take this test? Is your System 1 assuming that this test is going to be the same as last week's?*

Strategies to use #2: Harnessing the benefits of System 1

This chapter has explored the problems with the way System 1 thinks, but of course that's not the full story. System 1 is incredible: it's fast, effortless and it allows us to multi-task and navigate new situations with confidence. In many ways, it's the human superpower. It's also essential for schoolwork: the more students can answer accurately from System 1 responses, the easier they'll find things, the quicker they'll work and the more they'll be able to reflect on or extend their answers with System 2. Moving a response from System 2 to System I takes repetition and practice, but it's well worth it.

All of this can be used to motivate students, using comments such as these.

- *You need to know this material like 2+2=4 – we need to get it into System 1.*
- *Once you've got this in System 1, it's all going to feel much easier so let's keep practising.*
- *Repetition, repetition, repetition: it'll be worth it, because that's the way to get this into System 1.*
- *It's feeling difficult because there's a lot of System 2 in the mix: which bits can we practise separately so that System 1 can take over?*

Strategies to use #3: Learning to use System 2 to correct System 1's biases

Once students are more familiar with the characteristics of System 1 and System 2, it's easier to work out when to pause and think more carefully about something, bringing in System 2 to correct the in-built biases of System 1.

As teachers, we can prompt students to do this, embedding habits that will help them avoid the potential pitfalls of System 1. We can do this with prompts such as the following.

- *You've just said you're going to fail: that sounds likes a System 1 comment. Let's use System 2: which bits are you worried about, which bits are you less worried about?*

- *OK, so you don't want to talk about why you feel worried. That's understandable. Evaluating whether or not something is going to go well needs System 2; that can take a lot of effort and, when you're feeling tired and stressed, it's probably the last thing you want to do. How about we meet up tomorrow morning when you're feeling fresher and I'll help you think through where you are with your work?*

- *I know you're worried about this exam because your last test score was disappointing. That's a natural System 1 response because you're generalising from one situation to another. Let's use System 2 to explore why this exam might be different.*

- *You're telling me that there's no point revising: that sounds like a System 1 simplification. Let's think more carefully about this: let's think about what the value of each bit of revision is likely to be.*

Learning to recognise the limitations of fast-thinking System 1 and being ready to use slow- thinking System 2 to generate a more nuanced understanding creates a more balanced, healthier perspective on any situation. It helps students avoid the risk of catastrophising a situation and losing perspective. The good news is that, like any type of thinking, it improves with practice and gets easier and quicker over time.

> *That type of thought – the* I've done really badly *thought – comes more when you really care about the test. I remember when I did the entrance test – someone else said it was so easy – I remember there were a couple of questions I didn't understand – I thought* oh my god, I didn't get those questions, I'm

not going to get in, it's going to be the end of the world. *I knew I'd done a lot of preparation, it made me feel even worse. If you care a lot, it makes those thoughts worse.*

Year 13 student

Anyone and everyone benefits from learning to use System 2 thinking to override the simplified thoughts from System 1. But for teenagers there's one extra ingredient in the mix: the development of their brains means that balanced, nuanced thinking is harder for them than for adults. Balanced, nuanced thinking requires integrating several factors into one idea; it involves thinking through a range of perspectives. It's the difference between a small child's understanding of *goodies* and *baddies* and a more mature understanding that people don't fall into neat categories like this.

Balanced thinking rests on the capacity for sophisticated conceptualising, but the conceptual, integrative capacities of the brain are functions that develop over time; neuroscience has shown us that adolescence is the developmental phase when this type of integrated, conceptual thinking really starts to take off. This means that practising System 2 thinking is particularly important for adolescents: as Chapter 4 will discuss, helping adolescents to think in a broader, more nuanced way will help their brains strengthen the capabilities that will then shape their thought processes for the rest of their lives.

Areas for action

- If students talk about their work in blunt generalisations – *I'm always stressed, I'm rubbish at Spanish* – explaining fast-thinking and slow-thinking responses will help them understand why they think this way and why it's often inaccurate.
- If students don't want to talk about their exam nerves or they can't understand why they feel so much pressure, explaining the priming and coherence biases within our quick-thinking thought processes will help them see why sometimes we respond in a way that is hard to understand.

(cont.)

Areas for action (*cont.*)

- Are your students trying to apply their GCSE experience to their A level courses? Taking the time to explain the differences will help prevent the false expectation that they will be able to work the same way for A levels as for GCSEs or that the next set of exams will feel the same as the last set of exams.

4 Adolescence

Teenagers feel very bad about themselves a lot of the time.

Child and adolescent psychotherapist

Starting points

Adolescence is a key stage in brain development. This chapter will outline the physical changes that take place in the brain, explaining why these can lead to intense emotions and why it is important that we help students learn to think about feelings and outcomes in a considered and balanced way.

A key developmental phase

As Chapter 3 discussed, our responses are shaped by multiple past experiences. Interestingly, however, it is not the case that every past experience carries equal weight. Neuroscience is teaching us more and more about neuroplasticity, the brain's ability to change. It's possible to understand much more now about the brain's developmental phases and the ages at which dispositions get embedded most deeply. Early psychology focused on the intensively formative phase of early childhood, but more-recent research into brain development has shown that the brain goes through a second major formative phase during adolescence (Blakemore, 2018). Patterns embedded during adolescence have a long-term impact. If we can help teenagers find a calm and balanced relationship with assessed outcomes at GCSE, this is likely to roll forwards into their relationship with outcomes at Key Stage 5, university and beyond.

Understanding the mental rewiring that takes place during adolescence can help us unpick some of the causes of exam stress and work out how to address them. Dr Daniel Siegel is a clinical professor of psychiatry at the UCLA School of Medicine and the executive director of the Mindsight Institute. His books have done much to develop everyday understanding of the changes that take place in the brain during adolescence. He writes in an upbeat way about the importance of adolescence as a time to be nurtured, not endured, highlighting the difficulties of this intense period of change and also the opportunities available to embed healthy mental capabilities and processes (Siegel, 2021). Two ideas from his work are included in this chapter:

- the intensity of emotions during adolescence and the importance of thinking about feelings
- the need to help teenagers develop the ability to think in a balanced way, factoring in a long-term perspective and meaningful personal values; Siegel labels this type of thinking 'gist-thinking'.

This chapter will also explore how the natural push away from parents during adolescence means that there is a particular role for teachers to play as trusted adult role models. When it comes to understanding the emotions that connect with school work, many teenagers find it much easier to listen to advice from their teachers than their parents.

The parents will say that the kids say you don't know this, you can't help me with this. This raises the stress levels massively – the parents are worried but they don't feel like they can help. I'm sure this plays into the level of stress that our kids feel as well. There's this focus that it's only my teachers who can help me.

Assistant Head Teaching and Learning

Key takeaways

- Adolescence is an important stage in brain development: the habits formed during GCSE can last a long time.
- During adolescence, we need to help teenagers learn to develop a long-term, balanced perspective, centred around values that are meaningful for them.
- Students sometimes find it easier to listen to their teachers' advice about school than their parents' advice.

Questions for reflection

- What types of exam-habits do GCSEs encourage? Do students find it easy to let go of these habits in Key Stage 5?

(cont.)

Physical changes in the brain

Chapter 1 explained the tripartite model of the brain, distinguishing the brain regions that control basic bodily processes such as breathing, the brain regions that drive our instincts and feelings as a herd species and the regions in the brain that allow us to think about and choose our actions. During adolescence, the brain's prefrontal cortex – a key part of the rational, decision-making brain – undergoes major remodelling.

This remodelling involves reducing the number of basic cells by discarding the cells that are not used; this is why it is much easier to develop a particular skill if someone gets started before adolescence. The remodelling also involves improving the connections between neurons (Blakemore, 2018). By the end of adolescence, the brain works in a more efficient and connected way, allowing for thinking that is broader, more conceptual and more nuanced (Siegel, 2021)

The temporary consequence, however, of the changes in the prefrontal cortex is that adolescents experience emotions that are more intense and harder to calm. The prefrontal cortex has an integrative function, helping us balance emotional impulse with reflective, evaluative thought, calming our instinctive, emotional responses with a more measured thought process. The reconstruction taking place in this area during adolescence means that it can temporarily be harder for teenagers to combine thought with feeling, creating experiences that can feel sudden or out of control.

> *The exam stress – it hits suddenly – a couple of weeks before GCSEs I wasn't that stressed but then a week before, it set in. It was quite sudden – I suddenly felt like I had to get on it.*
>
> Year 12 student

As discussed in Chapter 1, the moments when we lose it or become hot-headed are the moments when the prefrontal cortex has stopped moderating the emotions thrown up by other parts of the brain. During adolescence, the emotional parts of the brain are more active than in children or in adults and – because the prefrontal cortex is under reconstruction – it can be harder for adolescents to regulate their feelings. As Siegel (2021, p.102) writes, 'without the calming influence of the cortical regions, sudden bursts of limbic lava and bursts of reactivity – the ancient reactions of fight, flight, freeze or faint – can emerge suddenly, sometimes without warning to anyone'.

I was getting 4s before – I didn't know if I was doing enough – I started panicking, so I just didn't stop revising. The panic started maybe a month before the exams.

Year 12 student

Key takeaways

- During adolescence, the brain undergoes major redevelopment.
- Adolescents often experience sudden surges of emotion.
- It is harder for the adolescent brain to balance emotional impulse with calm, rational thinking.

Questions for reflection

- Can you remember moments from your own adolescence when you experienced surges of emotion that felt overwhelming?
- Can you think of examples at school where teenagers are carried away by what they are feeling and don't seem able to think at all about what they are doing?

Labelling emotions: *name it to tame it*

The challenge of dealing with intense emotions is made more complicated for adolescents by the fact that some of these emotions are new. Adolescents can end up flooded by feelings that they do not understand. Sexual impulses are part of this, but so too are the emotions that centre around the evolutionary need to push away from parents. Developing an independent sense of self requires a degree of rejection of others: the angry conflict this often entails is painful. For teenagers, there is often an internal push–pull between the fearlessness or recklessness of the impulses that drive independence and the fearfulness of the vulnerability this independence opens up. Teenagers don't get to slip-stream behind their parents in the way they did as a child; establishing their own place in the pack can be fraught.

Name it to tame it (Siegel, 2021) has become a well-known part of therapeutic advice. Learning to label a feeling means that a teenager can talk about it and feel understood by others; as Chapter 1 discussed, social engagement – i.e. connection to others – is one of the most fundamental ways in which we feel safe and secure. Learning to label an emotion has an additional advantage: Siegel explains that using language in the context of feelings helps to bring the prefrontal cortex into the mix, strengthening the integration between emotional impulses and the calmer, steadier, more analytical parts of the brain.

As Chapter 1 explained, talking about fear, worry and anxiety is really important but it can be difficult for adolescents to do. Studies in the early 2000s (Rickwood et al., 2005; Biddle et al., 2004) indicated that young people have generally found it difficult to voice their mental-health concerns. There is encouraging data that suggests this is something that is improving (NHS England, 2018; Childline, 2019), but we should not underestimate the natural reluctance many teenagers face in being honest about times when they feel frightened or vulnerable. When it comes to fears about school grades, there's the additional difficulty of personal responsibility that Chapter 2 discussed: by the time students are in Key Stage 4, the idea that *they'd do better if they simply tried harder* may have embedded itself deeply in their psyche. It's difficult enough to admit feeling frightened and it's even harder if you feel it's all your fault.

> *I don't know what helps – but just someone being there – especially my mum – she doesn't understand how A levels work, it's not like she can help me with chemistry, but she's there and if I want to talk about it she'll listen. She's said that she won't judge me about whether I'm doing enough or not and that's really helpful.*
>
> Year 13 student

Learning the labels

Learning to use labels for feelings is important but it is made more complex by the range of labels that exist. *Unease, worry, stress, anxiety, panic, fear* – these are all subsets of the same basic threat-to-safety response, but they are very different labels and they suggest very different levels of emotion.

The sliding scale from *unease* to *fear* means that there's no neat way to assign the terminology. *Unease, worry* – these are natural, manageable emotions, which everyone experiences on a very regular basis; *anxiety, panic* – these are much bigger labels, implying an unmanageable experience, which may need medical intervention or professional psychotherapeutic help. The labels we use don't just allow a student to discuss their feelings; labels also carry implications about how to respond.

> *There's also a separate issue of the risk of overplaying the problem earlier on: if a child mentions that they are feeling anxious in Year 9, it needs to be taken seriously but not treated as if it's something massive, otherwise the child can end up believing that the anxiety is a bigger problem than it is and this can then become a reality.*
>
> Head of Year 9

Chapter 3 discussed the confirmation bias built into our rapid-response thought processes; if a child believes that they are experiencing *anxiety* rather than *unease*, they are more likely to notice details that confirm this. Labels can end up generating their own reality.

In the research for this book, I met with a headteacher of a school where instances of debilitating exam stress had noticeably decreased. He told me that fewer students were freezing on the thresholds of exam rooms or becoming overwhelmed at the prospect of assessments. I asked him what he thought had created this change. He told me that they had started talking about feelings on a planned, systematic basis and they stopped using anxiety as an everyday label for nerves. They talked about worry instead and worked on the idea that worry is a normal feeling, which everyone experiences.

Normalising rather than problematising a feeling is a core part of what builds the resilience to endure a situation. Feelings that are familiar are often easier than feelings that seem out of place or surprising; hardest of all are the feelings we believe we shouldn't have. Much of the advice in this book rests on the idea that preparing students for public exams is about more than practising content and question-types; it's also about discussing and understanding the feelings that are likely to arise so that these feelings don't seem so surprising and overwhelming. The *Strategies to use* section at the end of this chapter contains ideas about how to help students do this.

Within society, there are also too many big medical words going around – this makes it worse. We need to help teenagers understand that worry is normal: everyone gets worried sometimes – labelling with a big label like anxiety *can make it worse. If we all talked more about the fact that worry is natural, we are all worried, this would help. We need to help pupils build this resilience so that they can manage this feeling: we can tell them that it's natural to feel like this, but here's what to do if it gets too much. We need to help them know that it's OK to reach out for help. This will help them find the balance which works for them.*

11–18 Inclusion Lead

Key takeaways

- In adolescence, teenagers experience intense and sudden emotions.
- Learning the labels for these feelings helps a teenager understand their reactions.
- Talking about feelings helps engage the calming influence of the prefrontal cortex.
- The labels we use shape a teenager's relationship with their feelings.
- Normalising rather than problematising a feeling builds resilience.

Questions for reflection

- When a teenager is worried about something they feel responsible for, what helps them feel able to speak honestly?
- Getting a sense of perspective on a situation can be tricky: how often do you hear teenagers use labels in a way that might be exaggerated? Do they describe a teacher as *mad* rather than *a bit annoyed*? Do they say they are panicking when in fact they are feeling on edge or unsettled?

The need to be seen-safe-soothed

We've got 50% pupil premium – there's a lot of deprivation in the area. We're dealing with domestic abuse, drug and alcohol abuse, child exploitation – these are the realities of the community we're working with. For a significant minority of students, that is their reality. Then they're sitting in front of us, trying to learn the difference between photosynthesis and respiration and they're dealing with all these issues. For these kids, school is an extra pressure on them. There's a fine line between talking about school being their routine and their safe space, and the reality: if they think they're failing at school, then it's not their safe space in the same way.

Science teacher

Daniel Siegel argues that, like small children, teenagers also need to feel seen, safe and soothed. They need to know that an adult cares about them, can protect them and will be able to offer consolation. In the push–pull conflicts of adolescence, however, the feelings of seen, safe, soothed can be much more complicated to achieve than in the early stages of childhood: falling off the swings and waiting for an adult to swoop in and kiss it better is easy in comparison with the emotional rollercoaster of the teenage years. For a teenager, some of the most frightening risks aren't solveable in the present at all; they're risks tied up with what's happening around them or with the fundamental question of whether the teenager feels they will become *enough* to be able to handle life as an independent adult.

In the context of exam stress, the seen-safe-soothed metric can be especially difficult to fulfil.

- **Feeling seen:** Who does the exam-stressed adolescent talk to about their feelings? Do they admit to their families that they think it's all going wrong, and risk anger and disappointment? If they are already in the *I don't care* disengagement spiral, how do they admit to themselves and to others that they do care after all? If they are hyper-engaged and on track to do well, will the adults in their lives understand their feelings, or will they unintentionally invalidate them by saying that *they've got nothing to worry about*? What does the support look like if they do open up? Hard-working or not, the go-to solutions often centre around the idea that the student should be doing something differently: implicit within this is the idea that *you're at fault here: you're feeling this way because you haven't done x, y and z.*

- **Feeling safe:** Are the results going to be OK? Getting to a place of safety doesn't happen until the results land and it takes years and years to break free of tests and exams altogether. Safety in the exam-stress territory is a long time coming and every student knows that tests get bigger, more important and more challenging as they progress through school.

- **Feeling soothed:** As Chapter 1 discussed, fear about grade outcomes arises from factors much broader than the actual grade itself. The sense of self-within-a-group and meeting the expectations of others play a big part, but teenagers are not only answerable to the other people in their lives. As Chapter 2 explored, teenagers also have to navigate the risk of their own internal anger: even if families and friends are saying *we'll love you just the same, we won't be angry if you miss those grades*, does the teenager feel able to be at peace with themselves when they find out their results? Will they have to handle the painful stabs of self-blame and a critical internal voice saying *you got it wrong, you should have made different decisions*?

Once the exams were all done, for three weeks I was happy, but then when the results were coming, I couldn't stop thinking about it, I couldn't sleep – I started questioning if I'd done enough revision – I didn't know if I should have pushed myself further – there was that doubt that I hadn't put in enough effort.

Year 12 student

Reducing isolation

Feeling seen-safe-soothed: this is difficult in the context of exam stress for all the reasons just discussed. It's not possible to remove the fear-factor of uncertain outcomes completely. But it is possible to deal with an adjacent factor: the feeling of isolation. As discussed earlier, the range of labels available means that it can be hard for a teenager to work out whether or not their experience is similar to someone else's. This can create a situation where teenagers feel alone or that others do not understand how they're feeling.

I feel like some teachers don't understand – their exams were so long ago. Parents too – it was different when they sat exams. I think my mum maybe wasn't putting enough pressure on me to revise. She kept telling me it didn't

Students are less likely to feel isolated or atypical in their feelings if they get the chance to talk about them in environments that they trust and with people who they believe can understand their perspective. This is why teachers can play such a significant role in helping students with exam stress. As teachers, we see students go through assessments year on year; our opinions are credible. We aren't their parents; there isn't the same evolutionary imperative to reject our advice.

This is why it is so important for schools to talk about exam stress in an open, calm and realistic way. We need to listen in a way that means students feel heard and understood. If we do this, we are more likely to be able to reassure them that their feelings are natural and help them understand how to handle their experience. If we can do this at an early stage, the more likely it is that these teenagers will develop a balanced, calmer relationship with the experience of assessment. *This is normal; people get through this; your exam result matters to you now but it is not the only thing that matters*: these are some of the most reassuring words a teenager can hear, and particularly from teachers.

Teacher validation has a massive impact. Sometimes when you get tests back, having one-to-one chats with teachers really helps – having the conversation, hearing the teacher proving that they are not disappointed in you, that they don't just look at you as a grade – this makes a big difference. One of my big anxieties is disappointing teachers.

Year 13 student

Key takeaways

- Teenagers need to feel seen, safe and soothed.
- This can be difficult to achieve in the context of worry about grade outcomes.
- We can help our students understand that their feelings are natural and manageable if we intervene at an early stage.

Developing balanced thinking and an authentic value system

Teenagers are often driven by short-term impulses: this can be terrifying for the adults around them to watch. Moving from a short-term focus, rooted only in the here-and-now, to a long-term viewpoint makes for much better decision-making. It's a core part of growing up (Siegel, 2021).

Siegel defines this shift as a movement towards *gist-thinking* and he argues that it is one of the most important parts of the adolescent brain's remodelling. Gist-thinking is broader and more balanced than the simple, short-term thinking of an impulsive child; it generates better decisions because it is more rounded and because it takes more account of long-lasting priorities and values. Gist-thinking plays its role in the exam-stress sphere as well: it helps to reduce the nervousness about outcomes because it enables a teenager to move beyond the all-or-nothing thinking discussed in Chapter 2.

The list below exemplifies the sorts of thoughts that gist-thinking facilitates:

- **A long-term perspective:** *GCSEs are a big thing right now, but I can see that they won't matter as much to me when I'm 30.*

- **A balanced sense of self:** *Everyone is talking about GCSE grades, but I know that there is much more to me than a grade list. I care about my friends, I'm good at cheering people up, I'm reliable: these are all things that will shape my life more than my GCSE grades will.*

- **An authentic value system:** *I can see that I want to do well because I care about making the most of the opportunities available to me, and I want my family to feel proud of me. These values are an important part of who I am, but I can see that GCSEs are not the only way to fulfil these values.*

If we try to map the idea of gist-thinking onto the System 1/System 2 view of the brain outlined in Chapter 3, we can see that System 2 helps develop our capacities to think in this broader, more balanced way. Using System 2 enables a teenager to intentionally factor in long-term considerations, wider aspects of their identity and their values. Like any part of the brain's capabilities, gist-thinking improves with practice; if someone practises it enough, it gradually becomes a System 1 reflex. As teachers, we can help our students develop gist-thinking if we ask them the questions that promote it. Examples of these are given in the *Strategies to use* section at the end of this chapter and the downloadable worksheet for *Strategy #2: Practising gist-thinking*.

Key takeaways

- Over time, teenagers develop gist-thinking: this means that they think in a more balanced way – they can factor in a long-term perspective and make decisions based on meaningful values.
- Gist-thinking improves with practice.
- As teachers, we can ask the questions that help teenagers develop their gist-thinking.

Questions for reflection

- What does your school do to encourage students to think about values that go beyond exam grades?
- What does your school do to help students work out the values and priorities that mean the most to them?

Strategies to use #1: Learning the labels and talking about exam stress at an early stage

At its worst, I've seen students who can't walk into an exam room because they are experiencing debilitating panic attacks and are lying collapsed on the floor. It can take 10–15 minutes for a trusted member of staff to talk them down to the point where they are potentially able to sit in the exam room – but sometimes they

A key theme in this book has been the importance of early intervention, helping students learn to manage the feelings about school exams in a way that prevents a build-up into acute anxiety. The comments above from a senior deputy head sum up why early-stage intervention is difficult: acute anxiety is obvious, it takes over, its grip so strong on the student that it is unmissable. Try to trace back a few years on the timeline; was it so obvious then? Can we really look around a Year 8 or Year 9 class and spot which students are the ones we need to help pre-emptively?

The answer, of course, is no. We can't. But that doesn't mean that we can't take action at an early stage: the key idea here is that unease, worry and nerves are things which everyone is likely to feel to some degree. Early intervention does not mean singling out individuals; it means helping all the students understand pre-test nerves. Early intervention is a systematic approach, not a matter of individual action.

Labelling, understanding and talking about feelings isn't easy because feelings are subjective and there are lots of labels; categorisation isn't neat and straightforward. For example, distinguishing *anger* from *jealousy* from *spite* doesn't involve a crisp set of dividing lines; nor is it easy to separate *happy* from *satisfied* from *content*.

Labels operate across two dimensions: they denote a qualitative description of what the feeling is and they also suggest a quantitative assessment of how strong the feeling is. When it comes to exam stress, we can help students develop their understanding if we remember to teach two separate things.

- **A qualitative understanding of the mechanics of fear:** As Chapter 1 explained, fear arises from a process that is instinctive. It's often reassuring for students to understand why it is they can't just switch it off; understanding this means that they don't feel it is some sort of personal failure if they can't follow the *don't worry* command.

- **The quantitative labels for the subsets or degrees of fear:** *unsettled, uneasy, nervous, stressed, worried, anxious, panicked, frightened.* These are the sorts of labels that help students conceptualise the different levels of fear-response.

Adolescence

Conversations at Key Stage 3 or early on in Key Stage 4 can focus on the milder end of the fear scale. At this gentler level, feelings are easier to understand and discuss because they are calmer: the lower emotional intensity means it's easier for the prefrontal cortex to do its integrative work and combine feeling with thought.

The important idea here is that a mild feeling of unease is still worth discussing: it's a bit like the proverb *save the pennies, and the pounds will look after themselves*. It's also a good opportunity to distinguish between mild and more intense versions of the feeling.

Questions like the following can help. A worksheet based on these questions is available as an online resource for download at bloomsbury.pub/exam-stress.

- *What does it feel like if you're just a little, tiny bit worried about something? What sorts of sensations do you get in your stomach, or your skin, or in your breathing? Why do you think your body is reacting this way? Can you explain what's happening?*
- *What labels fit with these little, tiny sorts of feelings?*
- *What is it useful to remember when you're feeling just a little bit nervous? What helps you feel steadier again?*
- *How can you tell if you're medium-worried about something? How does it feel then?*
- *What labels would you use for this medium-level feeling?*
- *What do you think are the external triggers that mean that your body has increased its level of response?*
- *Are you surprised by this reaction or does it make sense?*
- *What is it helpful to remember when you're medium-worried about something?*

If a student can use the beginnings of unease as an opportunity to understand why judgement can feel threatening (Chapter 1), why the agency/responsibility nexus is unsettling (Chapter 2) or why their quick-fire reaction might simplify the picture into an all-or-nothing evaluation (Chapter 3), they are much more likely to feel confident in their ability to manage this feeling. This develops their ability to navigate the experience and not feel overwhelmed by it. This in turn reduces the risk of escalation into something more acute.

Talking about feelings of worry at an early stage also means that it is easier for a student to reach out if things do get worse. Familiarity with labels that track different intensities makes it easier to check in with students about whether their nerves are increasing or not. At the far end of the scale, students with acute anxiety need professional medical and/or psychotherapeutic help and it's important for them to have the language to express this.

The importance of taking a calm and empathetic interest in pre-test nerves is a message that's useful for families to hear too. As Chapter 5 will discuss, conversations or attitudes at home inevitably feed into a student's emotional relationship with assessment. Families need to understand that mild levels of worry are indeed unproblematic, but this doesn't mean that the worry doesn't need to be discussed or understood. Talking openly about the possible reasons for pre-test nerves also means that families are more likely to understand how their messaging or attitudes can factor in. This is a theme that will be explored in more detail in Chapter 5.

Strategies to use #2: Practising gist-thinking

As outlined earlier in this chapter, gist-thinking involves
- a long-term perspective
- an authentic value system.

At school, students spend a lot of time hearing about the importance of GCSEs, A levels and so on. They also get a lot of practice in writing down the answer that they believe the examiner wants to hear. Unfortunately, this doesn't really help develop their ability to think beyond GCSEs or provide the opportunity for students to voice authentically what they think and what they care about.

Schools have to make sure that students take public exams seriously and the nature of mark schemes means that teaching-to-the-test is a fairly immovable part of today's educational diet. But it's still possible to help students broaden their thinking into gist-thinking if we ask questions such as those exemplified below.

A worksheet based on these questions is available as an online resource for download at bloomsbury.pub/exam-stress.

Developing a long-term perspective

- *GCSEs might feel like they are 100% important right now; we want you to take them seriously. But how do you think your feelings about them will change?*

- *How important do you think your exam results will be in 2 years' time, 5 years' time and 10 years' time?*
- *Why will the importance of your grades change over time?*

Developing a balanced sense of self

- *Your GCSEs will be on your CV, but why is this only part of what defines you?*
- *What else do you think is important to employers?*
- *What is important to you about other people in your life? Can you write a list of the things that matter that aren't GCSEs?*

Developing an authentic value system

- *What do you think? Let's forget about the mark scheme for the moment. What do you want to say about this and why?*
- *We're a school; GCSEs matter here, but this is only one part of what you do. What matters to you in other parts of your life?*
- *If no one else cared about your grades at all, how would you feel about them then?*
- *What are the bits of this situation that matter to you, rather than to other people?*

> *I tell myself it'll be done soon – I'll be able to do the things I want to do after it's all done.*
>
> Year 12 student

> *What does help me is things of substance – so, for example, applying for uni – working through things of substance – if you get this grade, then this is the option, if you get this other grade instead, then this is the option – this helps you see what the options are. Hearing what else is available and why it's still good – that's really helpful.*
>
> Year 13 student

Areas for action

- If a student opens up to you about how they are feeling about their school work, encourage them to think quantitatively as well as qualitatively about this feeling. If they are feeling worried, how intense is this worry?
- When you are talking about assessments, ask questions that encourage students to keep a broad viewpoint: ask students what matters to them beyond exam results.
- Adolescents can find it hard to take a long-term viewpoint and this can distort their sense of how important exam results are; verbalising how and why things change over time will help them learn to combine the short-term view with the long-term perspective.

5 External pressures

> *For the people who got stressed, I think it was pressure from parents to do well.*
> *Also the people who wanted to get into the sixth form but didn't know if they'd*
> *get the grades – that caused a lot of stress.*
>
> Year 11 student

Starting points

Family expectations, peer group influences, social media: teenagers are affected by pressures that come at them from multiple directions. Some of these external pressures are obvious, but some operate in a way that is much less explicit. This chapter will explore different types of external pressure, offering strategies to help students and their families understand these better.

Visible and invisible external pressures

> *It's not that I think teenagers shouldn't be aiming for high grades, the problem is*
> *that they seem to think high grades are the only way of achieving a happy life.*
> *Everything seems to be about a specific mark at the end: otherwise there is no*
> *alternative. This pressure feels so heavy. If you're in your 20s now it's harder: you*
> *have to work very hard to do well now: people are so career-focused because*
> *they don't feel there is any space to mess up. There is no space to make mistakes,*
> *to mess around. They can't just try this, try that. They feel that life is impossible*
> *without a plan and that without a plan they are a failure.*
>
> Counselling and Mental Health Lead

Chapters 1–4 focused on the causes of exam stress that arise internally from the physical structures of the brain. Exam stress, however, is not only driven by internal factors. *It's the parents, it's social media, it's the pressure from others, it's the cost of living, the job market has become so competitive*: when we talk about why a student seems worried about grade outcomes, external factors play their part.

In many cases, the external factors are obvious: Jonathan Haidt's book – *The Anxious Generation* – hit the headlines in 2024 with its compelling analysis that a life lived online is the major causal factor in the dramatic increases in general anxiety, depression and self-harm seen in adolescents during the last 15 years. As this chapter will explore, there seems little room for doubt about the role social media plays in leaving teenagers feeling overwhelmed by the scale, quantity and frequency of the demands made on their attention, sense of self-worth and time.

For exam stress in particular, often there are clear external pressures feeding into the situation. Any teacher will be able to provide anecdotes about families who are determined that their child reaches certain benchmarks; the senior leader's perspective below will ring true for many teachers reading this book.

> *The overwhelming issue for young people is this pressure that they have – it's like an arms race for the best grades. We are a big school and a large proportion of our students come from aspirational middle-class families. I think the biggest contributing factor is the attitude from the parents. We also see direct pressure from parents to kids: I was in a meeting with a student who is predicted a B at A level; they're working really well and I was telling them how impressed I was with their attitude, but their parent turned round and said* but they need an A to get into university.
>
> Senior Leader (Pastoral)

When families are determined for their children to do well, the pressure those children feel is real and difficult. At its worst it can lead to debilitating overload, a painful sense of failure or a lack of self-worth. But it is, at least, comparatively straightforward to understand because it is so explicit.

Not every academically anxious student, however, has a parent who is telling them they have to get an A. I have worked with many teenagers whose families clearly do not want them to be under undue pressure; the message they give repeatedly is *we just want you to be happy, it's your life, you should make the choices that you want.* For these students, the explanation for the pressure that they feel is elusive; they find it hard to make sense of why they feel as they do. In the absence of an obvious explanation, it becomes harder for the teenager to process their experience and steady the emotional impulses with the calming influences of the verbal, nuanced, more balanced parts of the brain.

Role models: conformist and prestige bias

Evolutionary theory explores how the human race developed into a species built around shared patterns of behaviour and knowledge and the ways in which this has shaped our instinctive impulses. Once our species realised that shared knowledge was its ace card in the survival game, evolutionary forces generated pressures which would drive us to learn effectively from others (Haidt, 2024). The thing about learning, though, is that it doesn't always require teaching: when it comes to human development, much of the learning takes place instinctively by copying others.

By necessity, families provide early role models, but as children grow up their evolutionary hardwiring drives them to look more widely; after all, there's no evolutionary guarantee that families will offer the best templates. Research suggests that there are two distinct processes by which we choose role models:

- **Conformist bias** drives us instinctively to copy what the majority are doing.
- **Prestige bias** is the impulse that drives us to look for the people society respects and take them as our role models (Richardson & Boyd, 2004).

Conformist bias and prestige bias each create pressures to be a certain way, whether or not anyone ever tells someone explicitly to do this. Both of these biases play their part within family dynamics, even when parents are telling their children that they *just want them to be happy* or *they shouldn't stress about their grades*. When older siblings are successful, conformist bias means that young siblings feel an inevitable pressure to copy that success. In families where parents praise other people's success – *she's got a place to do medicine, isn't that great!* – prestige bias kicks in. The explicit message may well be *we just want you to be happy* but the instinctive prestige bias means that the child believes that being a doctor, getting to a particular university, earning a certain amount of money are inherently more valuable outcomes than their alternatives. Family members who talk about how much they enjoyed their time at university or how great a particular outcome could be for the child inevitably create an indirect form of pressure, which bubbles along as an undercurrent no matter how often they try to avoid upping the ante in the grades-matter stakes.

In the absence of explicit, external messaging about the importance of doing well, students can end up feeling that their pressure is self-imposed. In some cases, this can make things harder: believing that pressure comes entirely from within binds it into a teenager's sense of self and it wraps it up in a layer of personal responsibility. It can also create a sense that it is inescapable: if it comes from within, then it's always there. The *Strategies to use* section at the end of this chapter provides some ideas about how to help students understand the external factors that contribute to their exam stress.

If we can help students learn to see the external factors that feed into this, we can help them make sense of their feelings. Just as importantly, we also help them create the space to start to delineate what other people care about, separating this from the things that matter to them. *If no one else cared about this, would I still feel the same?* This question can be transformative in helping a teenager begin to access an authentic understanding of their own values. As Chapter 4 outlined, an authentic sense of self is at the heart of a balanced, mature mindset (Siegel, 2021).

> *It's about meeting an expected standard. If you don't meet that standard, there'll be disappointment. In my own mindset, I have certain standards I set for myself – I want to prove myself to myself. If you're not meeting that standard, then you feel disappointed in yourself. You can't separate your own disappointment from the fear that you might disappoint others.*
>
> Year 13 student

> *For me, it's a self-imposed pressure; my mum is from a working-class background – both my mum and my dad believe that education is everything – but this is combined with* do what you like. *This creates a tension – I've got the freedom to make my own choices but I put pressure on myself to represent the whole family. I'm the first person to go to uni. There's always this pressure to make the whole family proud and make their funding worth it.*
>
> *I went to a private school – all my friends had parents who were doctors, lawyers, etc. Then my parents would say* you could be like that. *This makes it hard to be at peace with who I am – wherever I am, it's not enough. There's a pressure that comes with always being told that I've got potential. The unintentional message behind this is* you could be better, you could be better. *I find it very hard now to be still, academically, for a minute.*
>
> University student

Questions for reflection

- What is the prestige bias within your school? Which students get celebrated the most and why?
- Prestige is exclusive: only a few people manage to emulate the people who are praised the most. What does your school do to develop self-worth in the students who aren't getting celebrated up on the stage in assembly?

Behavioural theory: discover or defend mode

Young people need resilience; they need the capacity to take risks, to be able to handle making mistakes. I think there is just such a fear of getting it wrong, making mistakes, being judged for this. This can cause huge amounts of anxiety. This is in Years 8/9. Then in Years 10/11, when they get to exams it's the same fear of failure. Everything feels fear-laced.

Child and adolescent psychotherapist

In 2012, Nassim Taleb coined the term *antifragile* (Taleb, 2012). *Antifragility* is the idea that some types of strength need strain: trees need to be buffeted by wind to grow strong, our immune system needs germs, our resilience needs some adversity. *We learn through mistakes*: this is a statement that gets people nodding along in agreement, but it runs in opposition to our intolerance of mistakes on a societal basis. *They should resign! It's unacceptable! Kick him out! I'm not paying for this! I need a refund!* How ready are we to believe that someone can make mistakes and be acceptable all the same?

> *In general we are more risk-averse; parents are much more risk-averse. Students aren't taking as many small-scale, low-level risks – and so bigger events where the risks are higher, things that impact their future – they're just less prepared for these.*
>
> Senior Leader (Pastoral)

Societal intolerance of mistakes breeds wariness about risk: the best way to avoid mistakes is to strip away the risk that something might go wrong. This is the concept behind the label *safetyism* (Haidt, 2024). Jonathan Haidt's analysis of adolescent anxiety focuses on the impact of *safetyism*: he argues that teenagers are antifragile, they need to get things wrong in order to develop their self-belief. The type of confidence that rests on believing you'll get something right is a very brittle form of confidence; confidence that you can survive getting something wrong is a much deeper, stronger version. Advocates of free play and outdoor adventure argue that our increasing unwillingness to let children take risks in the outside world is a contributing factor in adolescent anxiety. When children lack the confidence that it'll probably all work out OK in the end, even if it does go a bit wrong along the way, anxiety can fill the space.

Haidt refers to two modes of behaviour: the discover mode and the defend mode. Our defend mode gets activated when we sense there is problematic risk in the mix; our discover mode kicks in when we think there is an opportunity ahead. Haidt argues that our defend mode inhibits personal growth: if we want adolescents to grow emotionally strong, we need them to be in discover mode. *Watch out! Be careful!* Comments like these trigger the defend mode. The trend towards safetyism in the outside world is obvious: newer, more cautious equipment in playgrounds, increasingly stringent health-and-safety requirements within institutions. Haidt advocates for a return to free play as a key anti-anxiety preventative measure: send kids outdoors without instructions, he says, with comparatively loose supervision, without the reminder to *watch out!* ringing in their ears.

Safetyism in the classroom

Possibly less obvious, however, is the comparable trend towards safetyism in the classroom. As Chapter 8 will discuss, the desire to help students succeed means we often frontload teaching with instructions about how to answer a question. *Don't forget to start with a quote! Make sure you use evaluative language! Use the sentence starter! Three points, please, not two!* These instructions are the classroom equivalent of *watch out! Two hands on the climbing frame! Don't go too fast on your bike!*

As Chapter 3 discussed, the brain's generalising, simplifying System 1 is whirring away invisibly in the background, drawing links between the moments when adults need to step in to prevent some sort of problem. System 1's tendency towards simplified coherence can end up equating *listen to my instructions in advance* with *you're not enough to be OK if you do it on your own.*

> *My teachers told me what to do and what to say.*
>
> Year 12 student

We need to think about the messaging in the classroom: does it activate the defend or discover mode? *Here's a question – see what you think – I'm looking forward to hearing how you want to answer it*: these words activate the discovery mode. There's an opportunity ahead for the child to try something new, learn something different. Front-loaded instructions, however, have a different set of implications. *We're going to practise our PEEL paragraphs today: here's your model answer, now let's follow that method*: the message behind these words is *you need to do it the way I tell you, you couldn't have worked this out for yourself.*

As Chapter 8 will discuss in more detail, we can't get away from the need to teach to the mark scheme and teacher-led instruction has its benefits: it's efficient, clear and it gets good results. But there is still the question of when and how often we do this. Do we need to adopt a *here's what you need to do before you do it* approach in Key Stage 3 as well as in Key Stage 4? Could we embed micro-opportunities for risk-taking in school work even at Key Stage 4, interweaving the equivalent of free-play opportunities into the work that we set? *Today we're going to do questions that don't have a mark scheme. Make a sensible decision on your own. Have a go and let's see what happens.* Within our current examination system, there will always be a need to teach to the test, but when we are helping students learn new content, is teaching to the test the only option?

> *GCSE was quite formulaic – especially e.g. sciences – you didn't have to understand, you just had to memorise answers. There's the pressure of playing*

the game. I do science subjects for A level – it hasn't been a big change in terms of room to do your own thing – you still need to understand what the examiner wants. You need to know what you need to write – learning the content isn't enough. Hitting the criteria is about 70% of what I think about. Maybe it's a 35–65% split, content:exam criteria.

Year 13 student

Key takeaways

- If we do not encourage young people to take small-scale risks, they do not get the opportunity to develop meaningful self-confidence.
- Meaningful self-confidence is the belief that it's possible to make a mistake and still be OK in the end; this is developed through the experience of making mistakes.
- Telling students how to answer a question before they do it is a form of *safetyism* and it is likely to limit students' confidence in their own decision-making.

Questions for reflection

- How often do you use mark schemes as a way to warn in advance? How often are students given the chance to think for themselves about how to answer a question?
- How often do students hear the equivalent of *watch out!* in the classroom?
- *Make a sensible decision on your own*: how often do students hear these words or their equivalent?

Social media

Social media plays a role: kids never get a break from it. They don't get to go home and stop. When I was at school at the end of the day I went home. This put a brake on it all. If I wanted to speak to a friend I had to pick up the phone and dial. There isn't this break from social media. As soon as the phone pings, there's the pressure to engage. This is relentless. We've got students who are up late, they're tired.

11–18 SENDCO

The impact of social media on mental health continues to be much discussed. Constant judgement, unattainable ideals of self-image, toxic and unrestrained vitriol: the opportunity for emotional damage is obvious. At first glance, however, the classroom experience might seem separate: social media might impact how happy a teenager is in general, but does it really impact their relationship with grade outcomes? I'd argue that the answer is a resounding *yes*, for the following reasons.

- **Time:** In the 2022 Pew Research Center report, 46% of American teenagers said they were online 'almost constantly' (Vogels et al., 2022). In the same year, the PISA global surveys of 15-year-olds (OECD, 2023a) found that 45% of students feel anxious or nervous if their phones are not near them. There's no reason to believe the UK statistics would be any different. Social media soaks up a huge amount of time. GCSE syllabuses have got bigger, it's harder to hit the top grades; concurrent with this it's never been harder for teenagers to feel that they have enough time for their schoolwork.

- **Distraction:** *We are forever elsewhere*; Professor Sherry Turkle, a psychologist and sociologist, summed up the impact of social media with these words (Turkle, 2015). The student sitting in a geography lesson may be facing the board, but at every buzz from the phone in their pocket, their attention is likely to wander. At home, the distraction is likely to be greater. Nicola Morgan – a popular writer for schools on mental health – opens her book, *Blame My Brain* (Morgan, 2013), with a description of a teenager intending to start their homework and suddenly realising that hours have passed in a constant stream of scrolling, clicking and responding. Her imagined case study is unsettlingly realistic.

- **Overload:** As the 11–18 SENDCo comments below, when there's too much to think about, some students just shut down. They are overwhelmed, unable to think or engage with what is happening at school. Too many platforms, too many comments, too many subjects: social media may sit to the side of what's happening in the classroom but it adds to the to-do list all the same. This is why the *Strategies to use* section at the end of this

External pressures

chapter offers ideas on how to support families in reducing the mental overload that social media can bring.

> *Teachers sometimes just get to see the outside – the child is sitting in their lesson, nodding along, the teacher thinks they're OK – but the child maybe is just thinking about all their homework, the different lessons that day, the test coming up, what their friends said on WhatsApp – they're functionally frozen. They look like they're engaged in the lesson but actually they're not processing it at all, they are overwhelmed by so much going on in their head. They're overwhelmed by all the competing pressures of everything that's happening that day.*
>
> 11–18 SENDCO

Pleasing others

> *On social media one group might start hating on another but you just roll with it. It's very judgemental, in all aspects of life. The way you dress – anything – you're never going to make everyone happy on social media.*
>
> Year 12 student

In addition, interactions online are likely to shape a teenage brain's sense of what it takes to meet expectations. Haidt's analysis of social media highlights the differences between in-person and online interactions. He describes in-person relationships as having more flexibility than online friendships. Typically, if we upset someone we know, we try to sort it out. It's unlikely to end the friendship irrevocably; we are more moderate in how we respond, and this means that mistakes are comparatively uncostly in the long term. In the online world, the reverse is true: online groups are easy to join but equally easy to leave. Within this context, social missteps have a bigger impact; people react in a way that is more dramatic than they would within an in-person relationship. This makes it harder to meet expectations (Haidt, 2024).

The idea of rigidity versus flexibility in meeting expectations is an important one. As Chapter 8 will discuss, the please-the-examiner culture for GCSE and A level means that exam success is a matter of pleasing someone else's expectations. Over time, mark schemes have become increasingly rigid. There's an upside to this – transparency and fairness – but the downside is what our generalising, simplifying thought processes do with this experience. *It's very likely you'll get something wrong, someone else won't agree with what you say*: this is the message that is coming at teenagers online and in the classroom. It's not really surprising that some teenagers find it so hard not to fear that they'll be found wanting in some way.

> *Maybe over 50% of revision is learning the mark scheme – I take drama – if you don't know how to write a question, then you actually get no marks even if you know the play really well. If you don't know how to write the answer, the revision is useless.*
>
> Year 12 student

Key takeaways

- Social media and near-constant phone use increases the pressure young people feel because it takes up their time, distracts their focus and overloads their to-do list.
- Expectations have become increasingly rigid in school exams: mark schemes have precise criteria. This can make teenagers feel that it's difficult to meet expectations.

Questions for reflection

- What boundaries are in place to help teenagers step back from their phones?
- Do anxious students believe that their answers will probably be OK, or are they worried that it won't be exactly what the examiner is looking for?

Strategies to use #1: Recognising external pressures

With parents, they are in the fear with the young person. I see this a lot. Parents have really understandable fears that their kids won't be OK, because things are so much harder than when they were growing up. They are in a place of fear and their way of managing this is to put pressure on their kids. They seem to feel the same rigidity that it has to go well.

Some parents say that they don't mind what their children get, but a lot of what is going on here is below the surface, it's unconscious. Parents do care about academic results, even if they say they don't, and children still pick up on the fact that parents want them to do well. Caring about academic success exists whether you're saying it out loud or not.

Child and adolescent psychotherapist

I think the most unhelpful thing that people say is what the parents tell their kids. Parents say that in order to progress certain grades are needed. This is the biggest problem I face: you will not get x job unless you get this grade in this subject. The incremental impact of comments said – maybe light-heartedly over the dinner table – gradually adds up. They are always trying to live up to what their parents think they need. I've had kids in tears saying that their mum will be embarrassed by what they get. Often this is the kid extrapolating from what the parents say – they've been told what to get to meet an aspiration and they interpret this as I'll be an embarrassment or a disappointment if I don't.

Boarding School Housemaster

We've got about 135 pupils in a year group: we've got a really broad cohort because we don't have a catchment area. Some have a lot of parent support – they've got all the revision guides, the parents are really invested; others don't have a school uniform.

11–18 SENDCO

Recognising external pressures is a key part of soothing anxiety. Understanding the pressure doesn't make it go away, but it does make it more manageable. As Chapter 4 discussed, when the verbal parts of the brain are engaged, emotional impulses calm down. Schools have an important role in verbalising these pressures and helping students – and their families – see them for what they are.

The families who put pressure on their children – overtly or not – are often the families who want to be supportive. They are the most invested, the most likely to turn up to parent–teacher meetings; schools have a role in helping families think about the messaging they are giving to their children. The following ideas will help students and their families view grade outcomes in a more balanced and flexible way.

- **Valuing character as well as grades:** Shiny grades and a clear run at a well-paid job make a big difference, but they are no guarantees of future happiness or wellbeing. Reliability, empathy, patience, kindness, cheerfulness, tolerance: there's a long list of personal qualities that matter far more in the long term than an individual exam result. Schools need to advocate for the importance of grades but it's possible at the same time to advocate for the importance of dispositions and attitudes. Families praise their children for good school reports; does school messaging via reports and reward structures encourage families to notice and praise personal qualities as explicitly as a clear-cut grade A in a maths test prompts them to praise academic success?

- **Balancing out prestige bias:** Aspiration is a good thing, but if schools only celebrate exceptional achievement, the picture gets distorted. Society needs many different types of people playing many different types of roles: pausing to celebrate and see the worth in non-exceptional moments helps to offset the instinctive prestige bias that one set of outcomes is inherently 'better' than another. Which students get celebrated, for example, in school newsletters? Is the spotlight typically on the students with the best grades or is there equivalent attention given to non-exceptional, everyday aspects of school life?

- **Advocating for the importance of a Plan B:** Rigidity and anxiety are natural partners. If something has to be one way, then there'll be more worry about all the what-ifs in the mix if outcomes go awry. Chapter 2 focused on external factors beyond our control: there's never a guarantee that Plan A will work out. Encouraging students to talk about the *what-ifs* will help them realise that if Plan A doesn't happen, that does not have to mean doom and disaster. *OK, so what if you don't get your grades? What does that look like? What are the options still available to you then?* It's equally reassuring for families to hear the same message from the school. Schools tend to celebrate their statistics about students who make their first-choice sixth form or university: do we message to a similar degree about students who had to recalibrate around an unexpected outcome and found out that Plan B had a lot to recommend it after all?

Strategies to use #2: *Make a sensible decision on your own*

Remember, confidence is not just about expecting to get it right. Confidence is trusting that you can make it through even if something goes wrong. This is why making mistakes is so important for developing meaningful confidence: the student who always gets it right gets no practice in recovering from getting it wrong.

Make a sensible decision on your own and then we'll discuss what you did: how often do students hear this? This instruction delivers two distinct messages:

- *I believe that you are capable of making a good decision.*
- *If you make a mistake, I'll be there to help you learn from it.*

It's useful to be mindful of the frequency of *watch out!* messages in the way we frame tasks. Not every piece of work has to be graded, not every piece of work has to follow mark scheme criteria, we don't have to give front-loaded instructions for every task. Exams, after all, are summative assessment; there's room for formative assessment along the way, which develops dispositions as well as subject understanding.

The emotional relationship a student has with their work is a key factor in their progress: encouraging moments of ownership and decision-making are just as important in the classroom as they are in any other growth area. *Here's a question: I'm not going to tell you how to answer it. Have a think and see what you come up with; then we'll discuss it. There are no assessment criteria for this one – it's just a chance to see what you think would work here.*

Strategies to use #3: Digital hygiene

The debate over how to protect kids online has been dominated by the question of which platforms or content teenagers get access to. Concerns about content are well founded, but there's a risk that they distract from the equally important question of how much time and energy is taken up by life online. *Sleep hygiene* is now a familiar phrase; we would benefit the teenagers in our care if we rolled out the concept to the digi-sphere as well.

A healthy relationship with social media needs boundaries. Putting boundaries around content and platforms is really difficult, but putting boundaries around time is – in theory – more straightforward. To be on their phone, a teenager needs access to their phone. Taking the phone away, turning off the Wi-Fi, shutting down a computer: these are physical boundaries that return teenagers firmly to the in-person world.

The challenge is the difficulty of choosing those boundaries. As Chapter 2 discussed, making choices – and carrying the responsibility for those choices – can be fraught, and especially so for parents and carers who have to answer the objection that no one else's families take their phones away. Schools need to make decisions about boundaries around phones at school, but the boundaries around phones at home are just as important: after all, it's using phones at home that keeps kids up late at night and it's using phones at home that can make it so difficult to focus on homework or revision.

> As a school we say they shouldn't have phones in school before Year 11, but we've got to understand the tech-tox: teenagers need to detox from this, but they've got fear of missing out. What happens if their friends are on and they are off? If everyone did the same thing, everyone stopped at the same time it'd be so much easier for them. Parents need to support them with this. There's also sleep hygiene – they're up late on their phones. For SEND, they often struggle with social relationships anyway and having everything going on constantly on social media the whole time makes it more overwhelming.
>
> 11–18 Inclusion Lead

When I first started teaching, classroom control was an isolated business. If students didn't behave in my lessons, there wasn't much back-up. Since then, schools have come a long way: it's now an established principle that good behaviour management requires consistency and several lines of support. Parenting, however, doesn't take place within the same sorts of structures.

Schools can really support families in working towards digital hygiene at home if they offer guidelines that they can refer to as back-up. There can be an understandable reticence about telling families what to do, but the fact is that if a teenager is in bed too late, they will not function well the next day. We all want young people to thrive; when it comes to digital hygiene, it's more likely to happen if we're all on roughly the same page. It's routine for schools to set expectations about uniform and equipment: if we want students to be ready and well equipped for school, then surely these expectations also need to include guidelines like those set out below?

- **Digital switch-off:** *We recommend no phones between 10pm and 7am.* Would this be a controversial message? Wouldn't it be easier for families to do this if their children heard the same message at school? *We ask you – as families – to sign up to our digital hygiene policy because we know that it will be much easier for your children if their friends are offline at the same time.*
- **Homework policy:** Online homework platforms are here to stay, but are we clear enough with families about whether students should use their phones to do their homework or not? Any digital device brings some degree of distraction, but homework without a phone buzzing every minute or so is a very different process from homework interspersed with notifications. We tell families what the homework is; do we offer equally clear information about the digital hygiene needed to support this? Do families have the answer they need when their children tell them they've got to be on their phone because they *need it for their homework* or because *they just realised they've got homework to do*?

> *Exhaustion is a big thing – at the very beginning I felt so much stress, but then as it went on I was really burned out – I ended up stopping caring – I put a lot less effort into it.*
>
> Year 12 student

Areas for action

- *But I've always wanted to be a doctor.* Are students blinkered by prestige bias? Encouraging students to invest in alternatives will help soften the *what-if* fear if they think they might miss their grades.
- Embed opportunities for students to learn that they can trust their own judgement when they are faced with an unfamiliar question: *make a sensible decision on your own.*
- *You should be in bed by 10pm; you should not have your phone in bed with you. You don't have your phones out in class and you shouldn't have them out when you are working at home.* Giving digital hygiene advice supports families in establishing healthy boundaries around phone use.

Suggested further reading for Part 1

If you are interested in finding out more about the ideas that have shaped this part of the book, the titles below are a good place to start:

Thinking, Fast and Slow – Daniel Kahneman (Penguin, 2012)

Nurturing Natures: Attachment and Children's Emotional, Sociocultural and Brain Development – Graham Music (Routledge, 2024)

Brainstorm: The Purpose and Power of the Teenage Brain – Daniel Siegel (Scribe, 2021)

The Anxious Generation – Jonathan Haidt (Allen Lane, 2024)

The Teenage Guide to Life Online – Nicola Morgan (Walker Books, 2018)

Blame My Brain: The Amazing Teenage Brain Revealed – Nicola Morgan (Walker Books, 2013)

A quick-reference summary of the material from Part 1 is available as a download at bloomsbury.pub/exam-stress.

PART 2

The journey through school: Strategies for each Key Stage

6 Key Stage 3: Thinking and talking about assessments

> *Emotional resilience work needs to be on the curriculum; they need these skills from Key Stage 2 onward. We can do this by talking about things that go wrong or talking about how they feel about things, about tests. If we did this at Key Stage 2 and Key Stage 3, they'd have the resilience in place to help them with Key Stage 4.*
>
> 11–18 Inclusion Lead

Starting points

But it's only a test! Are you surprised by how nervous some students are about assessment, even though exams in Key Stage 3 are comparatively low stakes? This chapter will explore how to help Key Stage 3 students develop a constructive relationship with exams and feedback, embedding habits that will support them as they move into Key Stage 4 and beyond.

Talking about assessments in advance

> *We see problematic stress from Year 7: there's a dichotomy between you as a teacher saying* don't worry it's only an end-of-topic test *and you as a teacher saying* pay attention, take this seriously, you need to know this. *We see it far more in female students.*
>
> Physics Lead

Whether or not students have experienced high-stakes assessments in their primary or junior schools, they will take their cues about secondary-school assessments from what key figures in their schools say. Let's think about what happens when Year 7 students hear for the first time about a significant set of assessments in a year-group assembly. To help explore the impact of different types of messaging, two different scenarios are given below.

In the first example, the head of year tries to downplay any potential negatives, encouraging students not to worry and giving a sketchy outline of what's ahead. The analysis that follows highlights how this type of approach can – perhaps counterintuitively – make students more nervous.

In the *Strategies to use* section, there is a different sort of approach, focused on the opportunities for growth and grounded in clear explanations, specific advice and a framework to help students understand what they are feeling.

An example of a year-group assembly: an approach that downplays the negatives

Year 7, I'm here to talk to you about your mid-year assessments. These are coming up after half-term, and we'll be emailing the details to your parents or carers. You don't need to panic about these. We want you to take them seriously but that doesn't mean you need to stress out about them.

I'm not going to say too much about the assessments now because I don't want you to worry or feel overwhelmed. Your teachers will be giving you lots of help in class to prepare for them, and we expect them to be something you can take in your stride.

Let's think about what this sort of messaging implies. Traced out below is a summary of what students are likely to hear when they process what is said.

- **These are coming up after half-term:** *Are they telling us now because I need to start doing something now? What should I do?*

- **We're emailing the details to your parents and carers:** *This matters! My family will care about how I do.*

- **You don't need to panic:** *Panic? What? These are going to be frightening? What have I missed? Are others panicking?*

- **We want you to take them seriously but that doesn't mean you need to stress out about them:** *OK, if I'm stressed, then I shouldn't be: I'm feeling nervous – does that mean I'm doing something wrong?*

- **I don't want you to worry or feel overwhelmed:** *There's a risk I get overwhelmed! But I'm not supposed to panic …*

- **Your teachers will be giving you lots of help:** *OK, but what does that mean? When is it going to start? Does it mean we'll be doing different sorts of lessons? What will they be like?*

- **We expect them to be something you can take in your stride:** *Does this mean they are supposed to be easy? But if we need lots of help from our teachers, then surely they can't be easy…? I'm confused.*

Looked at in this way, it's easy to see why some students start to feel nervous about assessments and why their brain's rapid-response systems start to interpret the situation as a potential threat rather than a positive challenge that will help them grow. The sketchy outline, downplaying the negatives and the mixed messaging all suggest that there might be something confusing or difficult about the assessments, or that the students' feelings are different from what is expected.

The *Strategies to use* section below offers a different way to approach year-group messaging.

👥 Strategies to use (year-group focus): Messaging about whole-year assessments

---

The following sample script is also available as an online resource for download at bloomsbury.pub/exam-stress.

An example of a year-group assembly: an approach that focuses on the opportunity for growth, specific guidance and a framework for understanding emotions

Year 7, I'm here because my role as your head of year is to talk to you about things that affect the whole year group. In three weeks' time, you'll all be doing end-of-year assessments, and I'm telling you about them now so that you know a bit more about them and can understand what they involve.

End-of-year assessments take place in each of your subjects. Your teachers will give you a piece of work to do on your own. Your teacher will mark this: your answers will show your teacher what you understand well and what you need more help with. This means that your teacher can give you feedback, which will help you with your learning.

These assessments are an important part of how we help you understand how to make progress. We expect you to take them seriously because we know that you want to do well in your schoolwork.

Your teachers will be explaining to you what sorts of questions will be in the assessments and they'll be showing you how to prepare. You don't need to do anything at this stage other than go home and tell your parents or carers about them. They will be delighted to see you taking a lead in telling them about your learning. If your parents or carers have any questions about the assessments, tell them that I'll be sending an email to explain, just as I have explained to you.

(cont.)

Now, as you'll know from our PSHE lessons, it's natural to feel worried or uneasy about moments when you feel other people will be judging what you are doing. Some of you might be feeling that way now. You might be feeling nervous because you have heard other people saying they get stressed about exams, or maybe you just feel a bit uneasy because this is something unfamiliar that you haven't done before.

Your form tutors will be checking in with you about this so there's an opportunity to discuss how you're feeling and get advice or support if you need it. You also know that I always like to hear from you individually, so if this is something you'd like to ask me about, just let me know and we'll have a chat.

The approach above gives a different set of messages because it achieves the following things.

- **A focus on the opportunity for learning:** Students get to see that the assessments are a positive chance to make progress.
- **Specific, boundaried guidance:** The head of year explains why the assessments should be taken seriously and then gives specific details about what will happen next, creating boundaries so students know when they have done enough.
- **A positive, achievable next step:** The head of year encourages the students to take the lead in taking the message home. This gives all students the chance to take a positive next step, building confidence that they can approach these assessments well.
- **A framework for understanding emotions:** The head of year creates a context that normalises exam stress, helping students feel unsurprised if they are feeling that way and confident that it's something the school understands, is calm about and can help them with.

Strategies to use (classroom focus): Pre-test classroom messaging

As a classroom teacher, you can use these principles as a planning grid to help you think through how you frame an assessment in advance. Below is an example of what this might look like in the context of an upcoming Year 7 assessed piece of work in history.

The following table is also available as an online resource for download at bloomsbury.pub/exam-stress.

An opportunity for learning	This assessment is a great chance for you to show me your work so that I can see how best to help you make progress. It also gives you an opportunity to practise preparing for assessments, and to understand how to learn from them effectively.
Specific, boundaried guidance	I'll be asking you to spend 20 minutes writing an extended answer about why William the Conqueror won the Battle of Hastings. To prepare for it, we'll be going through a fact sheet in our next lesson, discussing ideas. Then I'm going to ask you to spend about 30 minutes for homework on the revision task that I'll be setting. That's all you need to do at this stage.
A positive, achievable next step	We're going to begin by filling in this timeline about significant events in the run-up to the Battle of Hastings. I'm looking forward to circulating and seeing focused work: this will show me that you have an excellent attitude towards this task.
A framework for understanding emotions	Sometimes people feel nervous when we start talking about assessments: this is natural – it can feel like an unfamiliar situation and it's natural to care about the outcome. These feelings are likely to settle down if you know how to prepare for the assessment and I'll help you understand how to do this.

Feedback: *Am I doing well enough now?*

We've set up a feedback working group: we're pushing non-graded feedback. We know that pupils will not read the comment if they see a grade. The grade is the first thing they look at. Then the second thing they look at is someone else's grade. The comment will be the last thing they look at. From the moment they see that grade, they're focused on protecting their own ego. They want to know if this is a good grade or not a good grade. This can make them unresponsive to the feedback. We've been exploring delayed grading or not-grading but it's tricky because students want to see the grades.

Assistant Head Teaching & Learning

As Mental Health Lead in a large secondary school, I think about what people can be doing in classrooms. What would help the really anxious pupils would be to not name and shame people; asking them direct questions means teenagers feel exposed to judgement. Getting up, writing answers in front of people,

The central challenge with feedback is that the brain's tendency towards simple messages means that *here's how you could do better* is often heard as *you're not doing well enough now*. Formative feedback is an essential part of making progress but it can leave students feeling like however hard they try, they'll never fully succeed. This can be particularly problematic for high-achieving students, who were probably used to 'finishing' their work at primary school, getting 10 out of 10 in a spelling test or getting to the end of a reading book and moving straight on to the next one.

When teachers point out how my work can be better, it feels like they are saying that it's not good enough. Even when teachers also leave notes about what went well, it's easy to end up focusing on the negatives. I end up feeling frustrated because I try my hardest but it feels like it doesn't get the results I'd like.

Year 9 student

Strategies to use (year-group focus): Focusing on the reality of making progress

We need to help students understand the realities of progress so that they can learn that *here's how you could do better* is not the same thing as *you're not yet doing well enough now*. Learning to be realistic about progress can also help students feel less overwhelmed by what's on the to-do list.

Year-group assemblies can be a useful time to think about the following principles.

- **An opportunity for learning:** No matter how well someone is doing, there's always something to learn from an experience; an opportunity for learning does not mean something isn't good enough right now. *We focus on helping you learn from present experiences so that you develop a mindset that allows you to keep moving forwards and making progress. This doesn't mean that you're not where you should be for this stage in the curriculum.*

- **People always make mistakes:** *Sometimes people feel cross with themselves when they get something wrong, especially if they feel they could have got it right – that's natural; the important thing is to remember that mistakes are valuable if we are ready to learn from them.*

- **Progress is made one step at a time:** *Sometimes assessments can feel like there's a lot to do all at once. You can only do what you have time for, so we'll be thinking about what's going to be an achievable next step.*

The messages given by different feedback methods

As a teacher, it's helpful to separate out the different roles that feedback plays.

- **Summative:** This type of feedback defines the sum of how well a student is doing at that point in time. The headline grade – 90%, 80%, 70%, etc. – is summative feedback.

- **Formative:** This type of feedback is the advice that helps form future progress. *Revise parts of the heart the next time* is formative feedback.

- **Dispositional:** The way we feed back to the students shapes their learning dispositions, colouring how they feel about how well they have done and influencing their relationship with schoolwork both now and in the future. The feedback that shapes dispositions is less clearly defined than summative or formative feedback. This is because the dispositional feedback is often an off-shoot of how we present the summative or formative feedback. It's a matter of what the brain hears alongside what the teacher says.

The table below sets out some common approaches to feedback. It explores the dispositional feedback that these types of methods provide. The *Strategies to use* section later on will explore adaptations that can shift the dispositional feedback within these methods.

What gets said	What the brain hears
What went well… / Even better if…	There's much to recommend the principles behind the WWW/EBI feedback model: it aims to give balanced feedback in a way that doesn't overload. The difficulty is the framing. *What went well* limits praise to the bits that the student got right: it reinforces the idea that mistakes are problematic. *Even better if* are words that undercut the idea of what went well. They imply *Aha! You didn't do that well after all, here's how it should have been done.*
Traffic-light system: green, amber, red	The traffic-light system is designed to be a simple way for students to verbalise their own sense of their progress: green for the bits that are going well, amber for things that are less secure and red to highlight areas of concern. The principle of quick self-grading is constructive, but the framing brings other associations into the mix. Red messages *Stop! Danger! Don't move!* If a student defines their progress as red, the associative messaging means it's not surprising if they feel unmotivated, worried and stuck.
We'll focus on how to boost those grades even higher. Let's look at how to iron out those mistakes. Here's what you need to remember next time.	Future-focused messaging is an important part of feedback, but we need to remember that this perspective feels different to us from the way it feels to the students. As teachers, the 'future' is familiar: we know how it goes, we've taught this year group before, we know the route map that gets them there. None of this applies to the student: becoming something different in the future is inherently unfamiliar and uncertain. No student has the easy confidence that a teacher might have about ironing out those mistakes.

What gets said	What the brain hears
	Future-focused messaging compares the child to a future self that they have not yet become; it says *at the moment you are not enough*. It can cause angst because getting the question right the next time isn't as simple as, for example, *remember to add a teaspoon of sugar to this recipe the next time*.
	Growth comes in stages: children can't just choose to do it better; we have to help them practise and become the person who can do it. The advice about how to do it better is best given when the child is ready to do it in a different way.

Shaping dispositions for learning

For feedback to be constructive on a dispositional basis, it needs to help students understand the realities of progress. This means that the framing of the feedback needs to help remind students of the following principles.

- **Assessments are opportunities for learning:** Wherever anyone is on the summative scale, it's always constructive to be interested in the next step. The best, most constructive feedback focuses on what comes next, rather than lingering on past problems. *What do we do now?* is a constructive, forward-facing frame; *here's what you should have done differently* is backwards-facing and can feel tinged with blame.

- **We need to value present-time worth as well as future progress:** We need to help students engage their System 2 thinking (see Chapter 3) so that they can hold onto the complex thought that future progress does not mean the present-time reality isn't good enough for today.

- **We make progress by taking one step at a time:** If a student feels overwhelmed by the scale of what has to be done, they are likely to disengage and switch off. Formative feedback that focuses on an achievable, boundaried next step is much more motivating than general, unboundaried suggestions. *Write this equation out five times to help you learn it* is an achievable, boundaried next step; *revise your equations more* is unboundaried. Unboundaried, general advice makes it much harder for the student to feel that they can get it done; it is much more likely to make them feel that it's safer not to try than to put the effort in and run the risk of not meeting expectations.

- **Mistakes are inevitable:** *I knew that one! I should have got that right!* We've all witnessed the frustration students feel when they make mistakes. This frustration can be particularly acute for high-attainment students: they're usually accurate in their self- assessment – they could have got that mark. But the fact is that it's exceptionally rare to get 100%, even if a student knows all the material. No matter how hard they revise, in the heat of the moment, some mistakes will creep in. One of the most important dispositional lessons for high-attainment students to learn is that it is practically impossible to achieve the best-case output. There will always be moments of *aaargh, why didn't I spot that?*

Strategies to use (classroom focus): Reshaping the messages

At Key Stage 3, students become increasingly self-aware about where they sit in the pack. Assessments are – inevitably – a moment of judgement that crystallises a student's sense of their self-worth relative to someone else's. The comparison with others – or with an idealised conception of how they should be – can be really difficult. Key Stage 3 is the key stage where students most obviously begin to disengage or to hyper-engage, believing that the best way to avoid the pain of coming lower down the pecking order is to stop caring about that type of progress at all, or setting increasingly unattainable targets for themselves in their determination not to disappoint. If we want to help students develop a healthy, calm and balanced perspective about the realities of their progress, then the following shifts in messaging can be transformative.

Reshaping WWW/EBI

What if WWW/EBI were reshaped as different acronyms? How about using ATV for *aspect to value* and OFL for *opportunity for learning* instead?

- **ATV – *aspect to value*:** This shifts the focus onto finding something to value in the present. It's different from WWW because it avoids the implication that what went well requires a set of 'right' answers. ATV allows for praise that isn't limited to whether the answer was right. In an ATV model, the student who managed to sit still all the way through, or who arrived on time, or who didn't give up before the end can be praised, even if their summative score is low. The ATV model helps build self-worth even if high scores are never going to be on the horizon: it sends the message *see how you are now, let's see the value that already exists*.

- **OFL – *opportunity for learning*:** This sends the message that there's always a positive next step but it *doesn't* degrade the value of the present in the way that EBI does. It embeds the idea that mistakes really are valuable, because they help create the learning opportunity; it avoids the idea that the mistakes shouldn't have been there in the first place. In addition, it is a broader category than EBI. The OFL for a top-scoring student could be *recognise that some mistakes are inevitable, try not to be angry with yourself if these repeat*. For a middle-attainment student, it could be *saying my notes back to myself helped me remember the parts of a plant cell; I'll use this technique again next time*. For a disengaged, demotivated student, it could be *spending just ten minutes on reading my knowledge organiser will be worth it*.

Reshaping the traffic-light model

How about reshaping the traffic-light model into a high-/medium-/low-focus model instead? This model starts to teach students that they'll have to prioritise; it embeds the disposition that it's not about doing it all. It asks students to think about priorities within their own context, rather than judging them against the potentially overwhelming metric of *do you know it all really well yet?*. Even better, it allows teachers to remind students to limit the number of high-priority areas: *just choose one, keep it boundaried, Rome wasn't built in a day*. These are the messages that help prevent students feeling overwhelmed and shutting down.

At the other end of the spectrum, agreeing that something is low-focus is the antidote to hyper-engagement; rather than trying to keep everything in the 'green' box, spinning multiple plates at once, students are encouraged to slice some things off the to-do list, embedding the habits that will help them make a plan and shoulder the burden of responsibility for the Key Stage 4 revision process (see Chapter 2).

Retiming the forward-facing advice

Assessments show us, as teachers, where students need to do things differently, but we have a choice about when to give this message. Do we hand this over by telling them *here's how you should have done it* after an assessment, or do we log it in our planning notes and use it as a reminder to practise something before the next assessment? As teachers, it's our job to keep an eye on the future, but it can be gruelling for students to feel the pressure of having to get somewhere or be something they are not ready for yet. If we flip it round to the students' perspective, it's much more useful to get formative advice at the moment when you're actually working again on that thing.

The senior leader below comments on the idea of internal conversations: when we're marking work and messaging about progress, some of the feedback is really for us, internally, as teachers. This type of feedback is best made external at the point in the course when it is most useful for students, when they are ready to make that next step. If students have taken an end-of-topic test, some of the general, formative advice could be given when the class next returns to the material.

> As teachers we need to help lower stress levels – help students realise it's not as stressful as they perceive it to be. As soon as teachers mention stress or timelines, it can up the pressure. Teachers say things in class like we need to hurry up, you're not working hard enough or they show that they're worried about how well the class is doing. The internal conversations about how to do the teaching in the time available should remain internal but they often don't.
>
> Senior Leader (Pastoral)

Helping families respond in a way that is constructive

> This is an aspirational community – but it's not a community with the same experience of education themselves – or it's parents who were educated overseas or were at school here and struggled. They want something different for their children. There's a lot of frustration and anger when parents hear stories about how their children are behaving – we have some really tense parents' evenings. There's a disconnect between what parents expect school to be and what it's actually like.
>
> Assistant Head Teacher – Teaching and Learning

Within the student–family–teacher matrix, the teacher's perspective is exceptional. We're the only ones who are used to how things go; the flow through secondary school is familiar to us. Many families will be experiencing that phase of parenting for the first time. Unlike teachers, most parents or carers don't know what lies ahead, they don't always think searchingly about what counts as success/failure criteria for their individual child. Many are likely to feel defined by or responsible for their child's grade outcomes.

At Key Stage 3, schools have an important role in helping families understand the nature of child development at this stage. Parents and carers need to know that at this age teenagers are becoming increasingly alert to how they compare to their peers; this means that moments of judgement are bound to be nerve-wracking (see Chapter 1). They also need to know about how the physical changes in the adolescent brain can impact balanced thinking (see Chapter 4). This understanding matters because it helps to normalise what is likely to be a very unfamiliar experience for parents and children alike. Family members need to be unsurprised if their child finds school a challenging experience or if they don't always meet expectations. Families also need to understand why their children may find it difficult to explain how they are feeling.

> *What didn't help was other people reminding me that I needed to study. Also when people were trying to speak to me and I wanted alone time to de-stress, that wasn't very helpful. It doesn't help if your parents are telling you someone else is revising this much, you should be revising the same.*
>
> Year 12 student

Strategies to use (year-group focus): Guiding families' relationships with outcomes

Introduction-to-the-year events are a useful opportunity to help the families of Key Stage 3 students understand some key concepts.

• **It's more constructive at Key Stage 3 to be interested in what a child is doing than how they are doing.** Talking about what they are doing at school is one of the best ways for a child to process content, improve their fluency about a topic and deepen their engagement. Asking a child *what the test was on* actively helps with the learning process; asking a child *how they did* embeds the idea that outcomes matter to the parent, messaging to the child that test scores play a role in defining how the family views the child.

- **Exam stress can impede progress and it is comparatively common.** When I was interviewing teachers for this book, I asked for their estimates of the numbers of students affected by pre-exam nerves to a degree that was impacting their progress or engagement. The numbers varied depending on the academic intensity of the school, but the lowest figures offered were approximately 10% of a year group. The families of Key Stage 3 students can find it hard to understand how much pressure teenagers are under now: they didn't grow up in the maelstrom of social-media judgement and rigid exam-syllabus expectations. They need to know that the best way to calm pre-exam nerves is to help their children understand their feelings at an early stage. If their child says that they are worried about a test, families need to help them understand this feeling and normalise it, following the advice from Chapter 1 and reassuring them that it's natural to feel this way.

- **Their success as a family is not defined by their children's grades.** Empathy, taking an interest, patience and flexibility – these are all much more important parenting skills than producing a child who can nail quadratic equations. Families need to hear this message because – if there are conversations ahead about academic performance – they need to know that they will not necessarily be judged negatively if their child is not succeeding. Some parents need the school to tell them that developmental problems arise for the child when there are unrealistic expectations about what should happen next. Students are more likely to achieve their potential if their families are calm, engaged and supportive.

Strategies to use (year-group focus): Messaging within school reports

The school reports that I have seen have typically given families a guide for how to interpret or understand the report, but they have not given advice about how to respond. Again, there's a role for schools to play here, helping families to respond constructively by reminding them of the following principles.

- **Listen first, react second.** *They wouldn't understand*; this is the comment I've heard time and time again from students with fractured relationships with their parents. Often what they mean is *I don't think they'll listen well enough.*

Families should be encouraged to listen to their child's reaction before they comment on the report: *what do you think about this report? Is there anything you're surprised by? How do you feel about what this report says?* Creating space for the child to reflect on their report will help the child feel clearer about how they are doing and what they feel able to do differently; it also means that any advice the parent or carer gives next is likely to be a better fit for what the child needs at that moment.

- **No child wants to do badly.** If the grade outcomes are disappointing, it is likely to be more disappointing for the student, even if they don't want to show it. Parents who react angrily or say how disappointed they are take away the space for the child to acknowledge that they are disappointed too and feel supported rather than criticised. If children don't have the space to do this, the natural thing to do is to flinch away from the feeling, saying they *don't care* or *don't want to talk about it*. This is the beginning of disengagement. The first response to a disappointing report should be empathy and support: *it can be difficult to hear that things aren't going so well. How do you feel about this? Do you feel cross or unhappy? Let's think about how I can help you with this.*

- **Progress is made by specific, attainable steps.** Telling a child to *do better in science* or *behave better in class* or *make more effort* is too vague to be easily attainable. Most workplaces are familiar with the importance of specific, achievable targets: students' progress is enabled by the same principles. *It'd be a good idea to work on maths: how about 30 minutes at 6pm on a Wednesday when you talk me through what you did in class that day? 30 minutes sounds enough for the moment.* That's the sort of suggestion that creates a fulfillable expectation; it's much easier for the child to buy in when the boundaries are specified and they can see the finish line.

> I constantly felt guilty and overwhelmed. I felt too stressed out and overwhelmed to even open the textbook. It was like having a completely messy room and you don't know where to start to tidy it up – I had so much to do – I couldn't even fathom where to start. It's a massive fallacy that if someone isn't working, that means that they don't care. This isn't always true.
>
> University student

> You know it's serious – it doesn't help when someone else is telling you this – it makes it such a big thing – it's no different from the other exams you're doing

except it's being marked by people outside school. If you put it on a big pedestal, that creates unnecessary stress. If you're doing the right studying, it shouldn't be that stressful.

Year 12 student

Areas for action

As a year group

- Does year-group messaging present assessments as a constructive opportunity for learning, does it normalise feelings and does it offer specific, boundaried advice?
- Does year-group messaging explain the realities of progress?
- Do families receive advice about how to respond to school reports?

In the classroom

- As a classroom teacher, do you give specific, boundaried advice about preparing for assessments, focused on how, when and for how long?
- Is feedback framed and timed in a way that develops constructive dispositions?

7 Key Stage 4: The prospect of GCSEs

I'd say this to teachers and parents: put yourselves in that person's chair for ten minutes: how would you feel if that was you?

11–18 SENDCO

Starting points

Teachers and students are working alongside each other to prepare for GCSEs but their experiences are very different. It is easy to forget how far away and unfamiliar GCSEs are for teenagers. This chapter will explore how we can reshape the prospect of GCSEs in way that makes the experience more manageable.

The view from the other side of the desk

The view from the other side of the desk is different. This is an idea I come back to time and again when I'm thinking about teaching. Teachers and students: we're in the classroom at the same time but our experience is very different. When it comes to the prospect of GCSEs, one of the sharpest differences is that – as teachers – our timeline runs for a year at a time. We build up towards exam season safe in the knowledge that we only need to manage the tension around this for a year. Next year, there's a new cohort, another chance to *get things right*.

This one-year cycle means that it's easy to forget that from the other side of the desk GCSEs are a one-off event: they are students' only chance to self-define via a set of GCSE outcomes. In addition, for most students, the run-in to GCSE lasts three, four, maybe five years. *Welcome to Year 7! Before you know it, you'll be taking your GCSEs. Everything you do now counts towards that outcome.* I remember a student in Year 11 telling me that they heard this in their welcome-to-the-school assembly; they then carried that message for five years. By the time they got to the exams, GCSEs had been in view for a third of their life.

Things have changed in the way we teach. The Key Stage 3 curriculum used to be all about breadth and trying things out. Now it's much more a matter of preparing them for next steps. Lots of schools are starting GCSE courses in Year 9, so there's a truncated Key Stage 3. Increasingly they are no longer exploring and creating and dabbling at Key Stage 3; it's much more about getting ready for Key Stage 4.

I teach English: the Key Stage 3 curriculum has become a preparation for Key Stage 4. We now work in the style of Key Stage 4, doing a poetry anthology which will mimic what they'll see at GCSE. I think this change is geared to the pressure from league tables, driving results up. It means that the language we use with them is different: we're saying this is the sort of style you'll get in GCSEs. They hear this even from Year 9. They're being told straight away that they need to know what a metaphor is because they'll have to mention this at GCSE, they won't be able to write about a poem if they don't know this word.

English Teacher

The impact of bringing the future into the present

There's all the fear of what the future looks like: they don't know enough about what it'll be like – they don't have the overview – all they've got is the jeopardy. I think we create this great big terrifying thing out of GCSE. We do this in an attempt to make them take it seriously. I think the kids view it as this thing at the end that will be everything – it'll be the gateway to their futures. We tell them that relentlessly.

Deputy Head

Navigating the future as well as the present – this is something that is very present in our context. Education is your future – this is their one chance – it's what the families believe is the exit ticket, it's the chance not to have to live in this area anymore. There's a lot invested in education outcomes – it's parents wanting their children to have a life that they don't have.

Assistant Head Teacher – Teaching and Learning

The consequence of starting things earlier

Teenagers are different from adults. We know this, but we don't always remember it; there's a risk that we apply to adolescent education the principles that help us succeed as adults. For example, as an adult, if I'm preparing to do something, a longer run-up probably gives me a better chance of success. I've seen this principle affect curriculum planning time and again: *let's give it more time, let's start it earlier.* The problem is that for adolescents, starting things earlier means starting things younger and this is where the adolescent–adult difference bites. Starting things younger often makes it harder, not easier, because it means starting things before a child is ready for them.

Can a Year 8 or Year 9 student imagine their Year 11 version of themselves? Even at the start of Year 10, can a student imagine their end-of-Year-11 self? This question is worth pausing on. Do they know that by the end of Year 11 they'll have a relationship with syllabus content that is different from their experience of it at the start of Year 10? Is it even possible for them to have any real idea of how much more manageable the content becomes as the GCSE course progresses? Let's not forget that GCSE is their first experience of a two-or three-year trajectory: how could they possibly know in advance how similar or how different things will be at the end?

This question becomes really significant when we factor in the idea of confirmation bias from Chapter 3. Imagine a student at the start of Year 10, clutching their syllabus outlines, copies of incomprehensible jargon-filled mark schemes, their ears ringing with the repeated advice to *take it seriously because this will count.* It would be entirely natural for this Year 10 student to feel overwhelmed. The confirmation bias hardwired into our rapid responses means that once the nagging doubt that *this might be more than I can manage* sets in, their brain will be more likely to latch on to evidence that confirms this doubt rather than evidence that negates it.

In Year 10 at the start of the GCSE course it jumped from school being just going to lessons to the experience of every subject teacher giving a spiel about how these lessons are now the start of the GCSE course. It started to feel much more scary because it was not just learning for learning's sake: what we were doing at the start of Year 10 was connected directly to a set of exams in two years' time. This made it feel like everything you learn you have to fully understand right away. At that point you don't know what the exams are – you've never seen a paper, so you don't know what's going to be important, you don't know about

Why do we mention GCSEs so often?

It's worth unpicking the reasons why there's a tidal pull towards mentioning GCSEs earlier and earlier. Top of the list seem to be the following.

- **We believe it motivates students to work harder.** Every teacher is alert for the tactics that make students sit up and listen. GCSEs matter and mentioning them can – at the right moments – generate engagement, but it's not the only way to get buy-in. Too many references to GCSEs can make students switch off.

- **Superstructure methodologies aid learning.** It's good for students to know the overall framework before getting down to the detail. This is a principle that I support wholeheartedly: the memory needs something to pin information to (Sherrington, 2019) and it's much easier for a student to see their own progress if they've got some sort of route map in advance. But the superstructure methodology doesn't mean that we have to talk about GCSEs in the same way in Year 10 – or Year 9 – as we would at the end of Year 11. Phrasing and shaping need to be year-group appropriate.

- **It's reassuring for us as teachers.** Referring to mark schemes or handing out specification check-lists helps us feel like we're doing our job properly – *there it is, I've given it to you, we're on track* – but we need to distinguish between what we need as teachers and what the students need as 13- or 14-year-olds for whom the summer of GCSEs is still unimaginably far in the future.

- **We've got into the habit.** The biases within our brain make us creatures of habit. As discussed in Chapter 5, conformist bias means that instinctively we copy what the majority are doing. As a profession, we've been using GCSEs as the justification for taking school seriously or the explanation for why a question needs to be answered a particular way for so long that it's probably become semi-automatic.

Strategies to use (classroom focus): Focusing on the present

If we pause to think about it, it would be perfectly possible to teach without mentioning the actual GCSEs much at all in Year 9 or Year 10 and it would definitely be possible to teach to a specification without handing out material at an early stage which is fundamentally designed to be used by adult examiners at the end. Chapter 8 will explore in more detail when and how mark schemes get used as a teaching tool; this chapter focuses on the broad concept that reference to a far-off future is more difficult for the students as adolescents than it is for us as adults, for whom the cycle through to GCSEs is comparatively quick and familiar.

Pausing to think about the *future in the present* question invites comparison with wellbeing techniques designed to reduce the mental overload of distractions and split focus. Many schools have started to embed mindfulness techniques into their mental-health provision; surely it's time to think about what an educationally mindful approach would look like in the classroom? At the core of mindfulness is the principle of connecting to the present, not the future. It facilitates an integrated self, unsplit between the present and future: it allows for a better appreciation of the value that already exists.

As discussed in Chapter 6, acknowledging the value that is already there is a key part of building self-worth and reducing the risk that students unthinkingly equate *could be better in a year's time* with *not doing well enough now*. A *future in the present* approach keeps inviting students to evaluate their present progress by reference to the future goal; an educationally mindful approach keeps the focus on the present. It encourages students to think about the value of where they already are and to focus on what to do next rather than measure their outcomes by a yardstick that may be months or years away. A *focus on the present* approach, therefore, keeps things focused on manageable next steps and sets targets that are within reach.

The table below sets the two approaches side by side. It is also available as an online resource for download at bloomsbury.pub/exam-stress.

Aim	A *future in the present* approach	A *focus on the present* approach
motivate students to work harder	*Your GCSEs matter; you need to take this seriously because all this counts towards your GCSEs.*	*Learning helps you develop your skills; this school values focus in class because this helps you learn. Let's focus now so that we can learn today.*
justify how a question should be answered	*You need to use terminology like metaphor, alliteration, simile because your GCSE examiners will want to see this when you take your GCSE exams in three years' time.*	*Using the right terminology makes your answer better because the right terminology allows you to be more accurate in what you say. The three words we're going to practise using today are metaphor, alliteration and simile. Let's work on using these today.*
offer a superstructure	*We're starting the GCSE course today so I'm giving you a copy of the specification outline so that you can see what we'll be covering.*	*We're starting the GCSE course today, so I'm giving you a route map of what we'll be working on and when. I'm not giving you a copy of the specification because it's full of technical terms that you haven't learned yet. I'm giving you a version that uses language you already know. In due course I'll give you the exam board version but I'll do that when we're far enough along for it to make sense.*

An educationally mindful approach doesn't require any changes to schemes of work or types of tasks. As teachers, we will still need to plan what we do now based on where we need to get to in two years' time; as teachers, we'll still need to use GCSE mark schemes to inform the advice that we give. Within an educationally mindful approach, however, the explicit focus on the future remains internal to us, as teachers and as adults for whom that future is manageably close. The educationally mindful approach shifts only what we ask the students to think about and the framing we give to it: *focus on today, here's what to do next*. It's important for us as teachers to keep touching base with what the end goal looks like, but for the students – for the young adolescents for whom the GCSE season is much, much further away – it's much less overwhelming to focus on today and boundary the to-do list with manageable, achievable next steps.

The need to balance out the messaging

The other major downside to the years-long run-up to GCSEs is that the messages given bed in very firmly: *take it seriously, GCSEs are the gateway to your future, they're really important; you won't get a good job without them*. Roll forwards to Year 11 and a one-to-one conversation with an exam-stressed student where there's a temptation to flip the messaging to the opposite extreme: *they're not actually that important at all! They won't define your life – you don't need to worry so much about them*. This flip in messaging can be really difficult: the student has spent years being told they should care about GCSE outcomes; it's not easy suddenly to switch this off.

I think some of the messaging doesn't help – the messaging that your GCSEs don't matter, in 10 years' time they won't ask you about them, no one will care about your GCSE grades in 10 years' time – this feels like it invalidates the feelings. GCSEs may not matter in the future, but when you're doing them it's the scariest thing you've done so far – and they do matter now for the step-by-step process of getting to that future – they affect sixth form choice, university etc. They also matter for your own ego – they do matter because you want to do well, it's part of who you are to care about doing well. It's not helpful to hear they don't matter.

University student

Part of the problem here is that – as discussed in Chapters 2 and 3 – the brain gravitates towards simple messages. It takes a lot of mental effort to recognise the truth of seemingly conflicting messages: *either GCSEs matter or they don't – they can't matter and not matter at the same time*. Added into the mix is – as discussed in Chapter 4 – the difficulty many adolescents face in conceptualising the future or recognising that they really might feel differently in a few months' or years' time.

I think sometimes if you're with family they can undermine the exams too much – saying it doesn't define you. You've spent two years leading up to it – it's not helpful to belittle the exams.

Year 12 student

Strategies to use (year-group focus): Things change over time

When school decides it is appropriate to start talking regularly about GCSEs, there's a need to balance out the messaging and work on helping students remember the following things:

- **Value changes over time:** In the summer term of Year 11, GCSEs are one of the most important things for a student at that moment in their life; at Key Stage 3 or the beginning of Key Stage 4, there's no harm in flagging this in advance and it's certainly worth creating the space to empathise with the pressure that Year 11 students are inevitably going to feel when they are right in the middle of it all. But that doesn't mean that the prospect of GCSEs should be the most important thing in Year 7 or that students at the start of Year 10 should be working at the same intensity as at the end of Year 11. It also doesn't mean that the 20-year-old version of the Year 11 student will feel the same way about them retrospectively. *Think of something that was a really big deal in Year 5: it mattered to you then, it was important then, but do you still feel the same way now?* As discussed in Chapter 4, adolescents find it hard to blend these perspectives; they need our help in reminding them – frequently – that *yes, it's right to care about GCSEs in Year 11 – these things are important to you now – but things shift over time; it won't always feel this way.*

- **Different clothes for different seasons:** Preparing for GCSEs isn't like saving for a house. Going faster or getting ahead doesn't really get you anywhere. In fact, being exam-ready too soon is counterproductive; students get stale, it all becomes boring and repetitive. Students often feel pressure to be doing more, reading ahead in the revision guide, getting a tutor, etc.; families often think that doing a bit extra early on in the course is the secret to success. Parents – and students – need to hear that in Years 9 and 10, they should be focusing on the stuff they are covering in school at that time; they need to understand that the route to GCSEs has a fixed timeline and this timeline needs to be respected. Trying to get ahead with Year 11 content in Year 10 is like trying to get ahead by wearing a heavy coat in the summer. It's unnecessary, uncomfortable and – crucially – it doesn't make you any warmer when the winter comes.

- **The view is different at the top of the hill:** The route through to GCSEs is like climbing a hill. Students end up learning to do things that they did not understand at the start of the course. Like climbing a hill, it can feel difficult on the way up. When they get to the top of the hill, the hill is still the same – the GCSE content doesn't change – but the view does. As adults, this is obvious, but we need to remember that for the students, it's all new. Hearing this message will help to reassure them that if they don't feel exam-ready in Year 10, that's as it should be; they need to be patient and trust that step by step the view changes.

Separating teacher accountability from grade value for the students

The GSCE outcomes are the outcomes. They are the thing we get judged on. You get compared to other schools. When results are first in, schools are hot, phones are going. If you're seen as a top school, everyone wants to know if you've beaten them. My predecessor said that the fear you feel before results land, that fear never ever leaves.

Principal

One of the Year 13 classes I remember most vividly was a group of girls. They were all doing four A levels. Three of the students were hovering at the A/A* boundary in our lessons; none of these girls needed an A* for their university offer. All three felt overloaded by work and as the year progressed I could see how tired and worried they were getting. *OK*, I said to them. *You don't need the A* and you've told me that your other three subjects are the priority. I'll help you prioritise.* I put in place many of the strategies outlined in this book: I helped them boundary the time they'd spend on the homework I set, we quantified the value of different types of revision, I supported them in deciding whether or not their decisions and plans were sensible. After these conversations, there was a noticeable difference in atmosphere in the classroom. The students were more relaxed and – importantly – they were much more honest about what they found difficult; this allowed me to teach them more effectively.

When the results came through, however, all three got As, not A*s. I remember my reaction: I winced. I felt guilty: I'd legitimised this outcome. Should I have pushed them harder? It was my first year at the school. I knew I'd have a results review meeting in September with the senior leadership team. I could imagine the opening question: *what happened to the A*s?* What I couldn't imagine was quite how I'd answer it: whatever I might say would boil down to *I told them not to bother.*

I told them not to bother is a gross simplification: it's not really true – the nuanced answer was that I tried to help these students turn an overwhelming experience into something more manageable – but, as discussed in Chapters 2 and 3, the rapid-response part of the brain deals in simplified ideas. I still wince when I think of this story: I'm split between my beliefs about what was in these students' best interests and my concern about my own accountability. *We're going to get judged.* Come exam season, this is true for teachers as well as students.

> *Teachers are ultimately judged on their results, schools are judged on their results. We don't deliberately put pressure on teachers in this school – we don't say job and pay will depend on results, but teachers still want to do well for the kids and the school. It's quite intrinsic for teachers to feel this pressure. We want to send the kids out with the best results. Teachers know that they are going to have to stand by those results in September – they will be asked how their class did. Even if it's in a non-judgemental way, they'll still have to account for the outcomes. Also, no one is in this job if they don't care: there's intrinsic motivation.*
>
> Assistant Head Teaching & Learning

Two worlds operate in parallel in the classroom: teacher accountability runs alongside the grade outcomes for the students. One of the challenges of teaching is that we have to keep both of these in mind; the difficulty is that they don't always pull in the same direction. In every school I've worked in, the school year has started with a speech about grade outcomes: typically the message is *thanks and well done but let's keep it up and do better.* At every data drop, every teacher is aware that their classes' grades reflect their performance.

The ideas in Chapter 2 apply just as much to teachers as to students: there are external factors we can't control, our agency only goes so far, *could have been better* does not always equate to *it's your fault that this happened*, but – like the students – our brains simplify the message. SLT advice about how to raise outcomes can warp invisibly in our minds into *if the outcomes go down, you've been negligent.*

> *I'm always a bit disappointed by results because I always think there are a few kids who I wanted to do a bit better. It's one of those jobs where you feel accountable for a whole load of factors which are not in your control.*
>
> Teaching and Learning Lead

> *I always say to teachers in end-of-year appraisals, if you can say hand on heart I've done everything I could to help this kid – if you've taken the horse to water and they don't drink, then you've done what you can. Grades can change: each year it's different children. You can't be held accountable for the fact that a 16-year-old didn't get out of bed in time for their GCSE or that they came home, had a massive row with their parents, there's no food in the fridge etc., and that impacted how they did in their exams.*
>
> Deputy Head (Quality of Education, Curriculum, Data)

Strategies to use (SLT focus): Messaging from the senior leadership team

> *There's also the question of how much is teacher stress impacting the children? What support are teachers getting around their wellbeing at exam seasons? There's performance aspects to consider: grade outcomes factor into performance review. Senior leaders need to think about what they are doing to help teachers manage this stress.*
>
> Education and Safeguarding Consultant

Students need their teachers to help them keep a more balanced perspective in view; teachers need their line-managers to do the same thing. Compare these two sets of messages from a senior leadership team for the start of the academic year: one offers a simple perspective; the other offers something much more balanced.

An example of a start-of year SLT message: a simplified approach

We're proud of our results – we've got some great outcomes here. Particular congratulations to the science department this year, who raised their average grade by 0.8: great results! Round of applause for the science team!

Let's go into this year with our heads held high, but determined to do our best by the students. Let's think about what it takes to raise outcomes: our top teaching and learning priorities this year are engagement in lessons, homework completion rates and rapid response to families.

On our learning walks as a senior leadership team, we'll be looking to see you use our classroom techniques: clear openings to tasks, zero-tolerance to disruption and eyes forward. We want you to be active about homework: if kids don't complete it, follow it up. Communicate with heads of year, communicate with the homework clinic and get those emails sent home to families. We know you're busy, but we're in it for the kids: attention to the details, caring about the marginal gains – this is what makes the difference.

An example of a start-of year SLT message: a more balanced viewpoint

The start of the academic year gives us the opportunity to reflect on last year's outcomes and shape our priorities and attitudes for the year ahead. We need to look beyond the headline grades.

If your classes smashed it, you're going to be sitting here feeling great; if the grades are lower than you hoped, you might be feeling a bit raw. I've been there: I've felt that personal disappointment plenty of times. Don't let those feelings drive the reflection process, though: leave those grades to one side for the moment. Similarly, if the grades were great, that doesn't mean that there's no need to reflect. Ask yourselves this: 'What did I do last year that was effective? If I can do one thing differently this year, what would it be?' If the grades were disappointing, this doesn't necessarily mean that you need a total change in approach. Remember, there's a lot in the pot when it comes to grades that you're not responsible for. Think about the lessons that you know went well; don't just think about the outcome. Bottle the ingredients for the best bits and use these this year.

Our three teaching and learning priorities for this year are engagement in lessons, homework completion rates and rapid response to families. In your department review sessions, we're going to be asking you to work out how to make these aspects priorities in your lessons. Time is finite – we all know this – so what shifts are you going to make to bring these three areas to the top of the list? Communication takes time: we want you to start your department discussions with where you are going to make changes to free up the time to follow up more on homework and to email families more often. Cutting back in other areas can feel difficult to do: as your leadership team, we're here to support you. We'll be asking heads of department to tell us their implementation strategy: we'll support you in carrying the responsibility for those difficult decisions about what will get de-prioritised in order to make engagement, homework completion rates and rapid response the priority.

What difference would it make to you, as a teacher, to hear a balanced message like this at the start of the year? It's worth comparing it to the year-group assembly scenarios in Chapter 6. The same ingredients are there: there's a focus on the opportunity for learning in a way that is not defined by grades alone, there's a framework for emotions, there's specific, boundaried advice, there's a focus on the positive next step. In the classroom, two worlds run in parallel but what it takes for us as teachers to feel calmer, more reflective and more open to learning is noticeably similar to what the students need too.

Areas for action

In the classroom

- Do we need to refer to exams as much as we do? Could we be more educationally mindful by focusing on what students need to do today, without so many references to a far-away future?
- Is there an alternative to using exam terminology to explain the route forwards? Could we set the route map using language that is understandable right away and only use the exam-board material when students are close enough to the exam for it to make sense?

As a year group

- We need to keep reminding students that things change over time and they need to work in a way that suits the present stage.
- We need to make sure families understand that there is no real advantage in getting ahead: it is better to respect the in-built timing of the GCSE courses.

SLT focus

- Teachers need support from the SLT in managing the pressures of accountability.
- The SLT have a role in messaging that development as a teacher should not be driven by grade outcomes alone.

8 Key Stage 4: Preparing for GCSEs

> During Year 11 it felt like – I don't know – very high pressure – like it was a long slog. It felt like there'd be no break – it's a long time. It felt scary and very lonely: there was lots of going to school, but it was more stressful at school – study leave was calmer. At school you're surrounded by all these students who are feeding their stress into other people.
>
> University student

Starting points

How many times a day does a Year 11 student hear something about the GCSE exam? How many times do you mention the exam or the examiner or the mark scheme in an average Year 11 lesson? How many times in a Year 10 lesson? What would it be like to be a student hearing this day after day after day? This chapter will explore the impact of the daily exam filter, inviting reflection about how and when to refer to exam expectations. It will also offer practical guidance on how to support students in managing their revision and expectations in the final run-up to GCSEs.

Turning down the exam-filter

> There's a lot of it at the moment: we're at the start of the summer term. It's all they're hearing about, all the conversations are about exams, teachers are talking about it all the time. The students are putting pressure on themselves and they're hearing about the exams all the time from everyone else. In the exam: they are probably hearing this three or four times a lesson and they've got five lessons a day. That's 20 times hearing those words a day – easily.
>
> 11–18 SENDCO

> *I'm an English teacher. When we're first exploring a poem we don't talk about exams, but as soon as we move towards a writing task it's hard to avoid referring to how to get marks. I know I use phrases like* get marks for *or the* examiners like. *That language creeps in all the time – comments about what the examiner is looking for. When we were at school we weren't drilled in success criteria. I don't remember anyone really mentioning what the examiner wanted.*
>
> English Teacher

Referring to the exam

As a profession, we have got into the habit of teaching Key Stage 4 through the filter of exam requirements. This is understandable: constant reference to the exam offers the following advantages.

- **Indisputable justification:** *Why do we have to do this?* Students ask this all the time. *Because it's in the exam* is an answer that doesn't get much blowback.

- **Clear relevance:** No teacher wants to face criticism that they did not teach the right content in the right way. Referring to the exam makes it explicit that our teaching is on track.

- **Exam technique:** The easiest way to practise exam technique is to do practice tasks that replicate the exam and to talk about exam requirements on a regular basis.

- **Avoiding complaints:** Students and families have become so used to the need to teach to the test that if we don't mention the exam, there's a risk they complain: *but you haven't told us what's in the exam! When are we going to go through the mark schemes? What does the GCSE paper look like?*

> *I notice myself referring to the exam even though I don't want to – I've been an examiner, I'm so used to thinking about exam criteria – I notice myself saying* in the exam, here are the three success criteria – *it's an ingrained habit – it's hard to shift.*
>
> Head of Chemistry

The problem is, though, that running everything through the filter of the exam requirements colours the experience that the students have. It can make the process seem more nerve-wracking for the following reasons.

- **Pleasing the examiner is complicated:** As teachers, we're dealing with one subject at a time. A geography teacher knows what the geography examiner wants. But the students face multiple examiners across multiple subjects and – if you sit down and compare the mark schemes for different subjects – different examiners want different things, even in tasks that seem similar.

- **Learning the mark scheme is an additional challenge:** Students need to learn content *and* what to do with it. Both these things are necessary in our current exam system, but there's a question of sequencing. We need to teach exam technique for sure – that's indisputable – but do we need to do it concurrently with developing knowledge and understanding? Should we be talking about success criteria from the start of a course, or is it an end-game requirement, to be factored in after students know and understand the content?

- **Mark schemes create rigidity:** Mark schemes and model answers create the impression that there is one way to do something. This is inherently nerve-wracking because there's little room for manoeuvre. One of the symptoms of problematic anxiety is an all-or-nothing mindset and the belief that there is no Plan B: the exams have to go well. The exams do have fixed requirements – we can't change this – but there remains the question of whether or not we want adolescents to absorb the daily message for two to three years that success has to look exactly like this one way of answering.

For me personally, the GCSE content isn't particularly difficult. What's much harder is pleasing the examiner – it's like 'the examiner' has kind of turned into a sort of deity that's staring down at us. Finding a way to please the mark scheme is much harder – this feels about 50% of what we do – learning the exam paper. We talk about mark schemes and level ladders so often. Mark schemes are really inaccessible – the first time you read one it sounds like gibberish. There's so much jargon. They're not designed to be learning tools. So we spend a lot of time just trying to understand what the mark scheme is saying.

Year 11 student

Meeting expectations and pleasing others

As Chapter 1 discussed, teenagers are hyper-alert to whether or not they are pleasing to others. Their brains are constantly trying to gauge the best way to do it. One of the difficulties for today's teenagers is that pleasing others is much more complicated now than 20 years ago: social media means that social networks are bigger, interactions don't stop when the child goes home from school and the way others react is much less restrained online than in person. Running in parallel with the increasingly difficult social arena, pleasing others in the classroom has also become more complex.

Pleasing others has always been complicated – and it always will be – but the better we know someone, the less nerve-wracking it becomes. Familiarity removes uncertainty and it's easier to feel like we know where we stand. Unfortunately for Year 11 students, when it comes to pleasing others, *the examiner* takes up a large amount of air time and the examiner is difficult to please. Different criteria for different subjects; sometimes exacting, sometimes less so; the examiner is often looking for multiple things at once within one answer. From afar, the examiner seems powerful, capricious and fussy; the examiner communicates in language that is hard to understand. What's more, no school student ever gets to meet the examiner.

I remember teaching an exam class who were worried about whether or not their answers would be good enough. *Look*, I said to them, *I do examining; your examiners will be people like me. They're on your side; they're reasonable; they're realistic.* The faces in the room changed – I could see the relief. I left the classroom thinking *isn't it strange that saying this made such a difference?* I don't find it strange now: as Chapter 3 discussed, our brains whir away invisibly below the surface, knitting together experiences and creating simplified generalisations. Thinking about one examiner as a person similar to the teacher standing there in the room is not an inherently intimidating prospect, but the examiner as a concept – created by knitting together all the different references to examiners in general – is much more unsettling.

Strategies to use (classroom focus): Using a framework that is familiar and accessible

We can make preparation for GCSE much calmer for students if we rethink our messaging by staying alert to the inevitably fraught adolescent experience of trying to please others. The tables below unpick the messaging within two different approaches, one approach built around using an exam filter, the other approach rooted in keeping things familiar and accessible. The basic instructions are the same; the difference is in how they are framed.

Approach 1: Using an exam filter

Your examiner is going to want to see your calculation method written out in your GCSE exam – here it is in the success criteria in the mark scheme.

Who does the student need to please?	The student needs to please the examiner, but the student has never met this person; it is much harder for the student to feel confident about pleasing them.
Is it easy to understand what this person wants?	The language is technical and designed for examiners, not students; this makes it harder to understand.
Are their expectations fulfillable now?	The student won't know whether or not they have pleased the examiner until the exam results are in.

Approach 2: Using a framework that is familiar and accessible

In this department we love it when you show us you are thinking carefully through a question, so in this piece of classwork we're asking you to write down the sums you did to get to the answer.

Who does the student need to please?	The student needs to please the teachers in the department: these are familiar people – it is much easier for a student to feel confident about pleasing them.
Is it easy to understand what this person wants?	The expectations have been rephrased into everyday language that is easy to understand.
Are their expectations fulfillable now?	The expectation is fulfillable today; there is less waiting and less tension.

Strategies to use (SLT focus): A whole-school approach

At face value, the shifts in framing suggested above are not difficult to do, but using an exam filter approach has become deeply ingrained as a teaching habit. Changing habits often needs a really intentional focus, and SLT can make a big difference here by allocating enough training time for teachers to practise reshaping their instructions. In addition, it is much easier to embed this change if everyone is doing it; if one department keeps mentioning the exam and another department doesn't, there's a risk that students and their families start to question why they haven't seen an exam board mark scheme yet.

> *Why do we keep referring to exams? A lot of it is habit – we're just so used to teaching the exam through the process of the exam. We're just so used to doing it, it's hard to see that there might be a different way to do it. There's also a fear that parents will complain or SLT will mind if you're not doing exactly the thing that is the exam. The way to overcome this is that there have to be conversations about what are we trying to achieve at this stage.*
>
> Assistant Head Teaching & Learning

Strategies to use (classroom focus): Avoiding unnecessary complexity

> *I'd describe it as like sitting at your computer and you've ten tabs open at once, ten teachers demanding things from you: you can't cope with all that work. We have to step back and give them some space. Sometimes people find it hard to understand that.*
>
> 11–18 Inclusion Lead

Chapter 7 advocated *a focus on the present* approach. When we are thinking about how/when to refer to examiners, mark schemes and success criteria, we also need to think about whether we are keeping it simple or adding unnecessary complexity. At GCSE, students are juggling a large number of subjects, and expectations within these subjects have been increasingly specific and complex. It's no surprise that students often feel overwhelmed or as if they have run out of bandwidth.

As teachers, we want to do our jobs well and to lock on exactly to how to help students get the best grades they can. But we need to be careful that the ultimate complexity of the GCSE exams does not bleed into an unnecessarily complex route through. The metrics of keeping it simple versus adding unnecessary complexity are a useful way to unpick decisions about what to say about the exams and when. Some examples are given below.

Teaching decisions	Keeping it simple or adding unnecessary complexity?
teaching the mark scheme before a student does a question	This can add complexity: the student has to think about the differences between different types of answer before they've even had a go at getting familiar with what the answer might be. Why not keep it simple by getting the students to answer the question first in whatever way makes sense to them and then think about what ingredients in their answer make it?
referring to what the examiner wants	This adds the complexity of an unknown person: why not keep it simple and talk about what your department wants instead?
using mark-scheme language	Mark-scheme phrases such as *developed argument* or *evaluative language* add complexity because the words used are not everyday and familiar: why not rephrase into language that the students can understand easily?
talking about all the criteria for a particular band at once	This has to be done, but the question is *when?* Keeping all the criteria in mind is easiest once each separate criterion is already familiar. It's an end-game task: on the way through, why not keep it simple by focusing on one aspect at a time in practice questions, gradually building up to multiple criteria at once?
referring to what students will have to do in the GCSE exam rather than in this piece of work	This adds complexity because students have to think about the future as well as the present: why not keep the focus on the current task and talk about the GCSE exam when it is close enough to be easily visible?

We talk a lot in our science training courses about whether it's appropriate to give mark schemes to pupils. The mark schemes are written for teachers, not pupils. Here we will model an answer rather than give the mark scheme – we're using student-familiar language.

Physics Lead

Supporting students' decisions about revision

In our T&L discussions, revision is a big thing we're looking at. We're looking at the science behind memory and recall rather than just telling students just to go off and revise. We're trying to teach them how to use their memories, making sure they understand about spaced retrieval, the forgetting curve, that sort of thing. I worry a little bit though that in our efforts to teach students this early on we end up adding more worry than we need to. It's chicken and egg – we're responding to parental anxiety – we talk about how to do revision in Year 10 and we've introduced this earlier and earlier – even in Year 7. This is partly in response to Ofsted and parents – parents are more worried about outcomes now.

Assistant Head Teaching & Learning

How complicated do you want the revision process to be? This is a big question. As Chapter 2 discussed, revision used to involve an exercise book, perhaps a textbook, maybe some flashcards. There was comparatively little available and this offered simplicity. Now there's potentially overwhelming complexity. In addition, the range of revision resources available adds financial pressure into the mix: what happens when teenagers worry about whether their families can afford the revision guides?

We want students to revise effectively and in a way that fits their learning needs but how many of the following things do you want students to be thinking about at the same time as they are trying to remember how photosynthesis works?

- **Which resources to use?** BBC Bitesize, Seneca, YouTube, class notes, a revision guide, paper resources, additional materials on Teams or Google Classroom, etc.?

- **What to do with these resources?** Mind-maps? Flashcards? Quizlets? Practice questions?

- **Educational buzzwords** like *pomodoro method, spaced retrieval, the forgetting curve, dual-coding, fluency*?

- **How long to spend revising and when?** After school? In homework clubs? At weekends? Throughout half-term? How much is enough? How much is too much? What types of self-care should they be doing at the same time? If spending time with their friends and family matters for mental health, when is it OK to go out and for how long?

- **What to focus on?** What if they don't have time to do everything? When should they move on? What are the priorities? Do they need to revise the mark schemes as well?

- **Whether or not their family's expectations about workload and outcomes are realistic?** What if their parents are telling them they have to get As? What if their parents believe that all they have to do to make this happen is *stop being lazy*? What if their parents keep shouting at them to *get out of bed earlier* or *get off their phone*?

All of these things matter, but there is an obvious risk of overload if too much is in view all at once. As Chapter 2 discussed, shouldering the burden of responsibility for revision can be really difficult for Year 11 students. We can't – and shouldn't – strip all responsibility away, but we can make this responsibility easier to manage if we help them in the following three ways:

- keeping it simple
- keeping it realistic
- sense-checking the decisions.

The sections below explore these principles from a classroom, year-group and family perspective.

Strategies to use: Keeping it simple

Classroom focus: Straightforward resources

Do you recommend one set of resources, which are boundaried and where it's simple to see how much there is? It's much easier for students to plan revision if it's straightforward to see the size of the resources: it's easy to see how much there is to do in a paper revision guide, but much harder to get the measure of materials if they are online links where it's only possible to see the length once the student has clicked through.

Year-group focus: Simple principles

Different students learn in different ways, but the most important principle behind revision is to turn input into output; whatever students are revising, they need to do something with it. Passively watching videos on YouTube is less likely to be an effective revision method; much better is if the student takes that information and turns it into output, by writing summaries, creating flashcards, saying it out loud, answering practice questions or similar.

In year-group assemblies, ask students what they are going to do with their revision resources. Acknowledge that different teachers will advise different things for their subjects, but keeping a simple central message to turn input into output will help students know that doing *something* with the revision material is the most important thing. Mind-maps or flashcards? This might make a bit of a difference, but doing either one of them will be much better than doing nothing at all.

Family focus: Don't overcomplicate things

Lots of families worry about whether their children are revising in the right way, but this concern can add tension to the process and cause children to disengage or be reluctant to discuss revision with their parents or carers.

Rather than complicating the process by suggesting different approaches, families can help their children by supporting rather than questioning their decisions. *Input into output* is a useful principle for families to know as well: *if your child says they are going to revise for an hour, ask them what they'll be able to show you at the end of it. Will it be a piece of paper with five key facts on? Will it be four flashcards? Whatever the child says, go with it and then praise when it's done.*

It's much easier to adapt the method once revision is underway: worrying too much about what to do and how to do it is likely to make getting started feel too complicated to engage with.

> For GCSEs, when you start thinking about all the things you've got to do – there are so many things to do you can't do any of them.
>
> Year 12 student

Strategies to use: Keeping it realistic

> In form time we went through how to build a revision timetable, but no one actually talked through the number of hours. There was a sense that each teacher

thinks that their subject is the only subject; I found myself listening to the teacher's advice and thinking, yeah, if I just did geography then I could do all of that, but I don't.

University student

Everyone has different situations – no people are the same – no people revise the same – this makes it harder to know if you've revised enough. Some people can just do it easily, some people have to go over and over.

Year 12 student

Classroom focus: Realistic revision plans

Time is limited and students have to make choices. Ask your classes how much time they have available to give to your subject. Scale this up by nine or ten subjects and check that this is realistic; if it isn't, challenge them on it. Encourage them to err on the side of caution: *don't overestimate – choose something manageable and let's make a game-plan that fits within that. If you end up with more time, then great, you'll be ahead.*

Classes need to hear this message so that there is space to discuss what those choices might be. *What are your top three revision priorities?* This is a useful question; it is much more enabling than only talking about all the things that could be done in an ideal world. Talking about priorities allows the student to cut things back to a manageable size; this brings the positive next step more clearly into view and makes it easier to be motivated.

Year-group focus: Realistic conversations

How much time do students actually have for revision? Ask them to put a number on it; encourage them to be realistic about what can be done in the time. Unrealistic conversations with friends about revision make everyone feel worse, not better. It's more constructive to stay focused on a sustainable amount of time to give to revision and make sensible choices about what to do with this time.

🏠 Family focus: A realistic understanding

Revision is often boring, gruelling and nerve-wracking: sometimes families need to be reminded about how grim revising for exams can be. For students who find school difficult, it's a sustained process of rubbing your face in things you feel you can't do. For students who are on track to do well, it's often a tedious process of going over and over material: it's like chewing an orange – even if material tasted juicy and interesting the first time round, it rarely tastes that way by the time it's been chewed right through to the summer.

Families often worry about whether their children are motivated enough and the concept of motivation often blurs with the concept of enjoyment. Maybe their teenager finds it hard to get started: this is natural. Maybe their teenager is in a bad mood: this is natural. Keeping it realistic for families means reminding them that it is OK for their children to be annoyed by the process.

Supporting in a realistic way means acknowledging this: *yes, revision sucks sometimes, but we're cheering you on. Tell me your plan for today; when it's done you can do something more fun.* Realistic support is a matter of focusing on one step at a time and celebrating the small wins of that bit being done rather than over-emphasising the August results-day finish line, which is too far away to be motivating. *You said you'd do an hour. It's 7pm now; at 8pm I'll come back and you show me what you've done. If you're finding it boring, let out your frustration by telling me at 8pm the most boring bits. I am there for you and I know it's not easy.*

> *The main feeling during GCSEs? Bored – just the same thing every day.*
>
> Year 12 student

> *There's the anger – you're never going to be asked any of this in your job, you'll never have to do this in 1 hour 45 minutes in the rest of your life.*
>
> Year 12 student

Strategies to use: Sense-checking the decisions

> *My GCSE time was so bad – I deleted social media, I had no fun time, I didn't take the weekends off, nothing – from Dec to June – I lost so much weight that the*

Classroom focus: Ask about plans

Time, resources, methods, priorities: these can be difficult decisions. Ask students what they are going to do. Then ask them why they've chosen this. If it sounds sensible, tell them so. If it doesn't, help them think about why it isn't. When they've got a plan that sounds sensible, tell them that it sounds like a good one. Knowing that someone else supports their choices makes it much easier for an adolescent to feel calmer about those decisions.

Year-group focus: Aim for a sensible decision

No one gets a guarantee that their results will be fine. This is the raw, hard truth that fuels exam stress. The best anyone can do is to make sensible, realistic decisions based on what they know at the time. Year-group assemblies can help students understand that feelings of uncertainty are inevitable but they will feel much better if they think about whether or not their plan makes sense based on where they are now.

Encourage students who are feeling unsure to talk to their teachers; *we can't promise it'll be fine, but we can tell you whether or not you're making sensible decisions right now. This is all anyone can do. Remember, if it doesn't turn out fine, we'll be there to help you decide what to do next.*

Family focus: Sense-checking expectations

Schools have an important role in helping families sense-check their own decisions. Do they have realistic expectations for their children? Are they realistic about how hard their children can/should work? Are they being empathetic to what the revision process is like?

Changing a family's viewpoint isn't straightforward; realistically, most schools don't have the time for in-depth discussions with parents and carers. But schools can make sure that the messaging sent home to families encourages realism and they can also make sure there is room for students to tell teachers if families have expectations that are unhelpful. Telling a teacher won't strip this problem away, but creating the space to verbalise it and understand it will definitely make it easier for the child to navigate.

Navigating disappointment and uncertainty

> *The reason kids come to school is to get great grades. We want the students to get the best grades they can.*
>
> Principal

The statement above is uncontroversial; I doubt there's a single teacher who would disagree with it. But for the students there are two difficulties:

- What counts as great grades *for them*?
- Whatever they do, no outcomes are guaranteed: until GCSE results land there will always be uncertainty.

Come results day, some students will be disappointed. For some students, the anxious uncertainty they felt along the way will seem – retrospectively – like it was well-founded: *it didn't work, I didn't get the grades, I didn't do the right thing*. Disappointment hurts: interwoven with it is often a sense of guilt and an unsettling feeling of *other people will view me differently, I was foolish to hope it would be OK, I can't see what to do next, I'm not as good as I wanted to be*. There is no short-cut around this. But we can help prepare students for it by giving them a framework to understand it and see beyond it.

Strategies to use (year-group focus): Maintaining a balanced perspective

Year-group messaging makes a difference here: when we're motivating students to aim for the best grades they can, we can help them keep a balanced, nuanced perspective by reminding them of the following messages.

- **There are external factors you don't get to control:** *Whatever the plan, sometimes it works out, sometimes it doesn't. When it doesn't work out, it hurts, but it doesn't end there. There's always a positive next step, even if it's hard to see it for a while.*

- **Things change over time:** *Your GCSEs are important right now; if your grades don't work out, it's going to feel raw. But that feeling will change over time. Your life will still move forwards and your feelings about GCSEs will change as it does.*
- **Plan B can work out for the best:** *It's always good to have a Plan B. Maybe your Plan B doesn't seem as attractive as Plan A right now, but life is full of Plan Bs that turned out to be better. If your heart is set on Plan A, it can take time to adjust to Plan B, but if you keep an open mind and look for the positives, you'll find that they are there.*

I'd want all kids to know that they are going to make mistakes and that's OK; they'll learn from these. I'd say to them, please have a Plan B. If teachers talked a bit more about Plan B, about when they ended up with a Plan B because Plan A didn't work out and it was all OK, that would help: real world experience makes a difference – kids need to hear about this. When teachers share their stories, it really helps students feel that Plan B can be OK.

Sometimes we need to help parents feel better about a Plan B too. We're a school with a sixth form, but it's good for parents to know about what Plan B looks like if their child doesn't get the grades for sixth form. Parents need to think about what would come next if sixth form doesn't work – this would help take the pressure off. Parents need to know that you don't get written off if you don't get the grades – it's not all or nothing.

11–18 Inclusion Lead

Areas for action

In the classroom

- Do we need to refer to the examiner or mark schemes as much as we do?
- Is the framework for pleasing others manageable, familiar and within reach?
- Are we supporting students in the revision process by helping them to keep it simple, keep it realistic and sense-check their decisions?

(cont.)

Areas for action *(cont.)*

As a year group

- Do Year 11 assemblies help students accept and navigate the inevitable uncertainty of GCSE results?
- Do Year 11 assemblies help students understand how to move through disappointment if their grades are not what they hope?
- Is there room for students to talk about expectations that they feel they cannot meet?

Family focus

- Does messaging to families help them to be realistic about revision?
- Does messaging to families encourage them to support their children by keeping targets manageable and achievable on a day-to-day basis?

9 Key Stage 5: The transition to sixth form

I've had pupils turn up for the first lesson of Year 12 with the mark schemes already printed out. They're using a method that worked for them in Year 11 and they arrive in Year 12 wanting to go at things the same way.

History teacher

Starting points

You're not doing GCSEs now! How do we help students manage the transition from Key Stage 4 into Key Stage 5? Do we help them understand how and why their experience in the classroom is going to feel so different from the end of Year 11? Do we focus enough on helping them develop the skills that help them make progress in longer, more complicated types of work? This chapter will explore this transition and offer practical ideas on how to help students adapt effectively to new challenges.

The Year 11 to Year 12 transition

As Chapter 3 discussed, our brains automatically use previous experience to shape how we respond to a present-time situation. Year 12 is one of the most important developmental stages in the school curriculum: it's the first time students have really had the chance to self-define in a significant way via their choice of subjects and they often have increased levels of personal responsibility – especially if they are in a sixth form college setting. Sixth form is the gateway between school and the adult world beyond.

The challenge for students, however, is that when they start Year 12, their most recent academic experience is the end of Year 11. If GCSEs went well, the natural reaction is to consider the run-in to GCSEs as indicative of what it takes to do well at school. If GCSEs did not go well, students are likely to doubt that they've got it in them to make good decisions about schoolwork.

The end of Year 11, however, is fundamentally different from the start of Year 12. At the end of Year 11:

- GCSE content and expectations are familiar.
- Students have practised material so much that recall is comparatively quick and answering exam questions has become routine.
- Students spend the final phase of their preparation consolidating or polishing their material rather than building it from scratch.

In contrast, the start of Year 12 can feel like an unsettling lurch because:

- Homework tasks take longer; feeling *finished* does not happen as quickly and it can be much harder – even for the top students – to get high marks.
- New content is unfamiliar and students don't know what their A level papers will look like; they probably don't feel like they know exactly where they are going and what they need to do to succeed.
- Content is broader; students have to learn to blend together material from a much wider syllabus. As a result, answers come much more slowly.
- Students are likely to feel like they are less successful in their school work than they were at the end of Year 11.

It is natural and inevitable for students to feel more nervous when a situation feels unfamiliar; there's a risk that they disengage or that they try to use the approaches which worked at GCSE as a way to regain the sense of familiarity and control that the smaller, easier GCSE syllabuses offered them. As we know, though, roll forward to the end of Year 13 and it can't just be a rerun of the Year 11 experience; there's less lesson time relative to syllabus content, the effectiveness of the student's independent learning is a much bigger driver for success than at GCSE, the risk that they feel daunted and overwhelmed by the prospect of revision is much greater.

At the start of Year 12 I remember having surprised myself with my GCSE results – I didn't think I'd get those grades. I thought that to do the same for A level I'd need to work incredibly hard from the off. I thought about how hard I'd worked at the end of the GCSE course and I tried to replicate this from the start. I didn't think about the start of Year 10, I just thought I could maintain the intensity of the end of Year 11 all the way through sixth form. I burned myself out.

University student

This means that effective ways to reduce exam stress in Year 13 have their roots in what happens at the start of Year 12. As teachers, we need to help students understand that their previous experience in Year 11 probably doesn't offer them the best game-plan for making it through Key Stage 5 in a way that feels empowered, calm and familiar. Once again, we need to keep in mind the difference in perspective from the two sides of the desk. We know what Key Stage 5 involves because we're used to teaching it; for the students, it's their first time doing it. Student expectations will be guided by the messaging we give them.

Reshaping expectations at the start of Year 12

We run around at Year 11, put interventions in left, right and centre, and then 12 weeks later they rock up in a pair of jeans and we expect them to be independent.

Head of Sixth Form College

It's surprisingly difficult to notice the ingredients that make up something that feels normal: this is because our brains are efficient. We save our conscious, careful, attentive thinking for when we really need it; anything that is familiar can be dealt with by our rapid, invisible thinking because – as Chapter 3 discussed – this type of thinking thrives in familiarity. The brain likes to reserve energy where it can: it's very natural to operate on autopilot wherever possible without really questioning what we're doing.

It's a rare Year 12 student who has the emotional or academic maturity to pause and try to work out how to shift their approach between Key Stage 4 and Key Stage 5. After all, how could they? They don't know what is going to be valuable to them in the context of a set of exams that are two years away. *Getting a piece of homework done in one go* – ideal for Key Stage 4 but is it as important at Key Stage 5? *Knowing exactly how to answer before writing the answer* – perfect for a pacey GCSE paper, but is this going to help their development at the start of Year 12? *Using lessons as their main way to access content* – entirely reasonable at GCSE, but far less likely to work at Key Stage 5, where independent study is a much bigger part of the process. *Deciding to stop before the work seems finished* – this rarely gets praised at Key Stage 3 or Key Stage 4; it's counterintuitive for a student to think that it might be an important piece of self-care at Key Stage 5.

Strategies to use (classroom focus): Frontlining why Key Stage 5 will be different

I think the biggest shift in the whole school journey is at the start of Year 12: we as schools need to understand that pupils are A level students when they finish. They should be ready at the end. We can't expect them to start the course that way.

Deputy Head (Quality of Education, Curriculum, Data)

To help students reshape their expectations, we need to give them the opportunity to notice their assumptions about how they should work. We then need to help them pause and consider whether or not these are realistic for what lies ahead. These types of conversations establish the headline principles that will provide a reassuring frame of reference as students move through Key Stage 5. Setting out headline principles at the start helps students feel more confident in their decisions about how they are going to study effectively.

The framework below can be used to structure the conversation; the most important ingredient within it is starting with *what* and moving to *why*. Asking why something worked is the question that unlocks a student's ability to think reflectively about the framework they are operating in. This then allows them to notice more clearly the differences between the Key Stage 4 framework and what lies ahead of them at Key Stage 5. The tables below map out some sample questions.

A worksheet based on the following tables is available as an online resource for download at bloomsbury.pub/exam-stress.

Looking back to Key Stage 4

Starting with *what*	Moving to *why*
What advice would you give to the current Year 11 students about what works and what doesn't?	Why does this advice work? What is it about GCSEs that means this is a good way to approach them?
What do you wish you'd done differently last year?	Why do you think this would have made a difference?
What resources did you use for revision?	Why did you use these? Why didn't you need to use anything else?
What did you need to do during lessons?	Why was this enough?
What did homework look like?	Why did your teachers set these types of tasks?
What was it like at the start of Year 10?	Why was this different from the end of Year 11?

Facing forwards to Key Stage 5

Starting with *what*	Moving to *why*
What do you think Key Stage 5 will be like?	Why do you think it will be different from GCSEs?
What do you think you will need to do in between lessons?	Why do you think what you do in your own time is going to be more important?
What is it going to feel like to be starting new material that is harder?	Why do you think this is going to feel different from the end of Year 11?
What advice do you think last year's Year 13s would give to you?	Why do you think their perspective is going to be different from yours?
Look at the textbook we're using in class: what do you think you'll need to know from it?	Why do you think you're not expected to know all of it as well as a GCSE revision guide?

Taking time to notice the differences between GCSE and Key Stage 5 is really important. If we don't do this, it is hard for a Year 12 student to understand that *doing OK* feels different at different stages. One of the reasons that exam stress can build over time – and especially for students who are used to getting good marks – is that the default is to expect to feel the same way about their work at Key Stage 5 as they felt about learning simple facts in Year 7 or finishing the revision guide at GCSE. They can end up thinking they are doing badly because they are using a metric that no longer applies.

> *What's paramount in my head is that the thing the pupils fear isn't real: their perception of themselves isn't real – they think they are weak, that they can't do it, that they haven't learned enough. The stress is real, but the baseline for it isn't. There's a fiction in their heads about what they think they haven't done or they're not good enough.*
>
> Housemaster

Learning to think about how to get started and what to do next

> *We get hugely emotional responses to internal exams – a lower grade suddenly seems like the worst thing in the world – they can't quite cope with the difference between where they are now and where they are aiming to get to. They don't see that e.g. a Level 4 in a Year 12 IB assessment is a different thing from their ultimate grade. They see interim results as a judgement rather than a developmental thing where it's part of a process. We talk about learning zones and performance zones – we try and help them see that these are different, that during the process they are not in the performance zone, that this is a different thing and it comes at the end.*
>
> Assistant Head Teaching & Learning

Headlining the differences between GCSE and Key Stage 5 will help students understand that Key Stage 5 is going to feel different. The next step is to help them understand that Key Stage 5 is a process: how they feel at the start and how they are likely to feel at the end are two different things.

Getting started

I remember helping a Year 13 student once with their personal statement. The student was high achieving, applying to an ambitious set of universities. She typically came top in every class test, but when she turned up with her personal statement draft she looked miserable. *I just can't get it right,* she said. I looked at her and asked her why she was expecting to get it right first time. *I've never had to do a piece of homework more than once – I've always finished it first time round,* she said.

I remember saying to her that writing a personal statement is like trying to get up on top of a table. If you try to get up there in one step it's nearly impossible, but stand on a chair first and it's suddenly much easier. I told her to write a different sort of first draft: *don't focus on length or structure at this stage,* I said, *get as much on paper as you can, then it will be much easier to see how to refine it. The first draft won't look like the real thing: that's fine – it's a step along the way, it's bound to be different from the finished version.*

Afterwards I thought about how the table-chair analogy applies to other aspects of Key Stage 5 too. Teaching to the test means that teachers and students alike keep thinking about standing on the table: getting up there, being able to do the exam questions, that's the target. But much of the work in Key Stage 5 is in learning to look for the chair first, even if it looks different from the metaphorical table-shaped goal.

We've all taught students who freeze and just can't get started with a piece of work: the essay that doesn't get written, the coursework that is non-existent right up to the wire, the sheet of calculations where some questions are left entirely blank. *Always do something!* runs the advice: *something is better than nothing!* But doing something can be difficult for the following two reasons.

- ***Something* looks different from the finished product:** Model answers are like standing on the metaphorical table; *something* is like standing on the chair. If students know they're supposed to be up on that table, it's not always easy to look around and choose something else to stand on instead.

- ***Something* means sitting in the middle-ground of uncertainty:** *Something* isn't finished, it might be wrong. *Something* might be full of mistakes; it won't look like the nice polished model answer or worked example in the textbook.

Moving through the middle ground

When I was interviewing teachers in preparation for this book, the need to help students be less reticent about making mistakes was a theme that came up again and again. *The students are mistake-averse*, said lots of teachers.

As Chapter 5 discussed, safetyism is common at Key Stage 4. Students operate in a rigid structure, they learn to follow instructions, they practise routines; there's rarely much opportunity to experiment with how they do something. It's no surprise that they find it hard to be confident: as Chapter 10 will discuss in more detail, confidence means knowing that you can handle making a mistake; it means believing that you can make a sensible decision on your own. Prior to Key Stage 5, students haven't had that much opportunity to make a sensible decision on their own and see how it pans out.

> *Dealing with uncertainty is something they find really tricky. It's probably particularly manifest within our school because we are academically selective. They arrive having been successful and they have probably embedded strategies that aren't actually that helpful: they're not used to getting things wrong. They're not used to not knowing: if they haven't seen it before, they give up. It's a rigid way of thinking.*
> Assistant Head Teaching & Learning (Independent School)

> *We've been talking to the students about their attitude to mistakes. One of the answers that stuck with me was the idea of* why would you want to make a mistake? *Lots of the students said that people wouldn't put their hands up if they thought they wouldn't have the right answer.*
> Assistant Head – Teaching & Learning (Comprehensive School)

It's worth asking ourselves this question: in our lessons, do we focus on the end-point or the first step? If we're working through an essay plan or explaining a new type of calculation, do we aim to get to the end or are we interested in exploring what the first step or mid point might be? Getting to the end, writing the complete answer, that's the ultimate goal, for sure. But for many students the real challenge is getting started or dealing with the uncertainty that arises with only getting somewhere, not all the way there.

Teach to the difficulties: focus your energy on helping with the things that students find hardest or on the areas where making a change brings the biggest benefits overall. This is a useful, common-sense mantra for any classroom environment. *Getting started, doing something*: if the alternative is doing nothing, not putting their hand up at all, then learning how to get started and do something are some of the most transformational changes of all.

Strategies to use (classroom focus): Exploratory questions

Like most things in the classroom, the solution lies in getting the students to think about it. Imagine asking questions like those listed below: would it make a difference? Would it help students feel more confident – more familiar – with taking that first step? Would it help them believe more wholeheartedly that getting somewhere is valuable and that it's not all about the final destination? Would it help them realise that being able to do it by the end of Year 13 involves lots of interim stages that all look a bit different from their final exams?

Questions to prompt thinking about getting started and making the next step

- *I'd like you to spend an hour on this homework, but let's imagine you only had ten minutes: what would be the most sensible first step to take even if you haven't got time to do it all?*

- *Here's a passage of Spanish to translate: maybe you don't know half the words. What's the game-plan for getting somewhere, even if you know that there's stuff you're going to get wrong?*

- *Let's imagine that I've set you a calculation you can't do. I'm still going to want you to write something down. Why do you think I want that? Why do you think I believe that it's going to help you make progress even if it feels a bit demoralising and unpleasant to write down an answer you know isn't right?*

- *If you're going to write an essay, there are things you need to do before you're in a position to see what you're going to say. What do you need to do first?*

- *I'm setting you some dates from this timeline to learn: there are more than I think it'll be possible to learn in one go. You're not going to be able to learn them all: which ones will you focus on and why? Maybe you reckon you've got time to learn 10–15 dates from the list: which ones are they going to be? Why do you think I want you to practise not doing it all even though last year, in Year 11, I was telling you all to aim for 10/10?*

- *Here's a type of question that you've never done before. What's different about it? I'm not going to tell you yet what I think you should do. I want you to practise sitting in the uncertainty: I want you each to think about what you'd do as your first step – you're not going to know yet whether this step is going to get you to where you want to be – but let's be curious: what could you do? Why does this seem sensible? Are there any other options?*

> *Pupils focus on learning a particular method – they focus on routine expertise – this is the way I solve that particular problem. They then fall apart if they get something different – they don't have this flexible, adaptable thinking.*
>
> Chemistry Teacher

Understanding the reality of making choices

> *Not having a dream is OK. Not everyone has a dream. Sometimes I'm overwhelmed by the amount of options there are.*
>
> University student

Key Stage 5 is also different from Key Stage 4 because students have to make much bigger choices and they often feel that the consequences of these choices have bigger ramifications. By the time Year 13 students sit their exams, the choices surrounding university destinations have been in view for at least four terms, maybe five. For an 18-year-old, this is a long time to have become invested in a particular outcome.

As Chapter 2 discussed, making choices can be exciting. For most of their childhood, young people are limited to the circumstances they happen to be born in, the schools that are geographically close and so on: at Key Stage 5, if students are fortunate enough to be in a position of choice, what happens next is a big, new, open horizon and – up to a point – they get to decide their direction of travel.

It's natural for schools to be upbeat about the choice-making process: *pick a course that you love! Look at the websites: make sure you choose somewhere that is right for you and where you'll be happy. Find something you're passionate about!* We want students to be excited about the potential within their future and to be invested in working hard to make the most of this.

Upbeat institutional messaging about making choices is understandable but – as explored in Chapter 2 – making choices can also be nerve-wracking. For students thinking about university, this choice now comes at a really high price-point: there's a much bigger premium on getting the choice right. In reality there often isn't a dream option that the student feels passionate about. Even the most sparkling of options will have some bits that are boring and include some downsides.

As teachers, we need to be careful that the motivational messages about *pick a course that you love* do not get warped into *the choice that I've made is the only choice for me*. If we talk too much about finding the right option, the implication in the shadows of this can be *one option will work far better for you than the rest*.

Invest in a Plan B, your first choice is not all there is, missing your grades might shift your direction in the short term, but it doesn't dictate the rest of your life: this has been a core theme throughout this book. For Key Stage 5 there's an extra dimension that's worth including: *it doesn't have to be amazing to be worthwhile*. We can help students be calmer, more flexible, more adaptive in their thinking about their future if we make sure they are realistic about these choices and open-minded about what counts as *good enough*.

Strategies to use (year-group focus): Being realistic about choice-making

The table below maps out questions which can help make sure that students are not losing sight of the principles that establish a balanced, realistic understanding of making choices.

A worksheet based on it is also available as an online resource for download at bloomsbury.pub/exam-stress.

A realistic view of making choices	Questions to keep these principles in mind
No choice is perfect: there are always pros and cons.	• *What are the downsides to your first choice?* • *What are the upsides to your second choice?*

A realistic view of making choices	Questions to keep these principles in mind
When we make a choice about our future, we don't know in advance exactly what it will be like.	• _Can you remember how you felt when you were choosing your sixth form courses?_ • _Has sixth form turned out to be the way you expected?_
The difference between Plan A and Plan B can be smaller than it seems in advance.	• _What do you think it would have been like if you'd made different sixth form choices?_ • _How much of what you value or will remember about Year 12 is connected to the courses that you chose? How much is connected to other experiences that had nothing to do with this school or college?_ • _How much difference do you think it would have made to how happy you've been or where you go next if you'd chosen different things?_

Embedding the principle that one size does not fit all

In many ways, school is a gradual progression from uniformity to individualism. When I used to help out at a local primary school I was struck by the slick group-ness of it all: walking down the road in a crocodile formation, group hand signals that all the children would make at key transition points like focusing on the teacher and moving to silence. Degrees of group-ness continue at Key Stage 3 and Key Stage 4: broadly speaking, the curriculum is the same for everyone, often the students are wearing a uniform, there are group expectations for behaviour.

By Key Stage 5 the differences between students are much more obvious than at the start of Year 7: they are much more obvious to us, to families and to the students themselves. But, despite these differences, while students are still in the educational pipeline there are still fixed exam criteria and a fairly rigid process of selection for university which values some attributes more highly than others. _Am I enough, will I be pleasing to others?_ As Chapter 2 discussed, this is the instinctive fear that bubbles along under the surface of stress about school results. It's exacerbated in contexts where there isn't much room for manoeuvre or where there are rigid expectations.

For students at Key Stage 5, this means that there can be an increased tension between who they are and what their context expects them to be. As Chapter 6 outlined, the roots of confidence lie partly in recognising the value that is already there. Sometimes this means recognising that the external expectations are temporary, school is one thing, real life is another. What works well for one student doesn't necessarily suit everyone; different employers look for different characteristics in their workforce. The more we can acknowledge that school grades are not the only measurement for value, the easier it will be for students to find their self-worth even if their grades are not as they – or their family – would wish.

Strategies to use (year-group focus): Who cares about what?

When I think about exam stress it's individuals who come to mind. I had a pupil who had a lot of pressure from home – she had responsibilities for younger siblings – there were very high expectations on her. She'd been a high achiever all her life, but I think she got to a point where everyone else's agendas were weighing heavily on her. I think she had very little space to express herself – giving up in lessons was a bit like the only rebellion she had room for. We're in an area of acute deprivation. We find with some pupils there's a self-expression that comes with breaking free from the expectations from home.

Assistant Head Teacher – Teaching and Learning

If other people in your life had been indifferent to what you chose, how many of your choices would have been different? This is a big question: as Chapter 5 discussed, we're often so influenced by what others value that sometimes we can't see what it is that we care about individually. Separating others' opinions from your own isn't always easy; it's especially difficult for adolescents who are instinctively driven to find belonging within a group. As Chapter 4 discussed, finding and valuing an authentic sense of self is a central task of adolescence; we need to make sure there is the space for teenagers to see beyond the simplicity of *a one size fits all, this is the way you have to be* mindset.

What would you choose if no-one else had a view? This question is difficult and – of course – it is also unrealistic. Other people do have a view and young people have varying degrees of freedom to make choices without reference to the values or needs of others. But this doesn't mean that the question isn't important all the same: teenagers often feel much clearer and calmer about their decisions if they feel like they can understand and process the reasons behind them. The questions below can help create the space for students to think about what it is that matters to them, individually.

A worksheet based on them is available as an online resource for download at bloomsbury.pub/exam-stress.

Identifying the expectations of others

- *Describe the person you think the school wants you to be.*
- *Describe the person you think your family wants you to be.*
- *What sort of person do you think a potential employer will want you to be?*
- *What characteristics do you think society values at the moment?*

Identifying the values that matter to the individual

- *What characteristics do you value in your friends?*
- *What characteristics do you value in your teachers?*
- *If you were an employer, what would you value in an employee?*
- *Think of a time when you felt proud of what you'd done. What does this reveal about what matters to you?*

It can also be helpful to remind families that their child's values might be different from their own: if a parent had to guess their child's answers to the individual values questions above, would they guess correctly? If their child's answers were surprising to them, would they pause to take their child's values seriously? Schools often share PSHE material directly with parents and carers to discuss at home; would it be useful to send a sample set of questions home to encourage families to hear directly what it is that means most to their child and why?

It can be very difficult for families and teenagers to be on the same page: giving time to understanding what the different pages look like doesn't suddenly resolve things, but it is at least a first step. As this chapter has explored, getting somewhere is better than not engaging with the question at all.

Areas for action

In the classroom

- Are we creating enough opportunities for students to think about how and why Key Stage 5 is going to be a different experience from Key Stage 4?
- Do we spend enough time talking about how to get started and valuing getting somewhere so that students do not freeze if they don't think they can do it all?

As a year group

- Are we offering a realistic, nuanced picture of making choices, reminding students that it doesn't have to be amazing to be worthwhile?
- Are we encouraging reflection about the values, characteristics and actions that mean most to the students on an individual, authentic basis?

Family focus

- Are we reminding families to be interested in who their child is now, as well as who they hope their child will be in the future?
- Are families open-minded about the reality that the values that matter to them might be different from the values that matter to their child?

10 Key Stage 5: Moving on from school

We did get advice about what university would be like but it's hard to pay attention to the advice before you go – but I think the best advice is to know that it's not set in stone, you can change things.

University student

Starting points

When students leave school, what do they take with them? Is it only their grades? This chapter will focus on the skills, attitudes and habits that students develop, offering practical ways to help students understand these better and feel confident that they are ready for what lies ahead.

What do students think they take with them when they leave school?

When students step out from our classrooms for the last time, they take with them the habits and life-view that school has helped them develop. There's only so much we can do to help them in advance with the stuff that's coming next – it's tomorrow's story, not today's. But we can help them take stock and notice what they've already got in their bag which will help them manage whatever it is that is coming their way next.

When the support structures of school stop, some teenagers find it hard to adjust. Sometimes our commitment to doing our best by the students means that there's less space available for these students to notice the solutions they can find from within. In a classroom, the students face forwards, eyes on the teacher; sometimes they notice how the teacher has shaped their progress more than they notice what they did themselves. *Thank you – I couldn't have done it without you*: if I see these words on a thank-you card, I always feel a bit mixed because it's a distorted picture. I want to say *stop right there – don't lose sight of the fact that it was you who did it. Make sure you pause to notice what it is that you did.*

Unlike the other chapters in this book, the strategies in this chapter are more backwards-facing. They are designed to help students notice what it is they have done already so that the skill set they take with them beyond school is clearly in view. Probably unsurprisingly, this chapter makes little mention of grades: the focus is on helping students see the learning that lies beyond the grade and understand the dispositions that will help them deal with stressful situations in the future.

> *At school we do everything we can to support pupils – and we run around doing this and that and then we send them out into apprenticeships, university or work and they've got to become independent. Some find this a problem. One thing I've seen – and this is anecdotal, I don't have sets of data for this – the more support they get at A level, when those pupils go off to uni, the anxiety or going off the rails can happen when the support goes away. It's as if we've delayed all this through our support measures and then it hits them when they leave.*
>
> Interim Principal

Confidence

> *The* believe in yourself, you're the best, you've got this *mantra is unhelpful – it's applied mindlessly – like a yoga instructor saying* well done for showing up *– it sets too low a bar for self-worth if you have always been told to be aspirational.*
>
> University student

Is *confidence* on your school website? I'm guessing that the odds are high it will be. Confidence is a super-power. It allows young people to be go-getters, to aim high to reduce the restrictive fear they might feel about trying something new.

But it's also something that is often majorly misunderstood. *Believe in yourself; you've got this*: in this everyday messaging, the implication is that in order to be confident you have to be likely to succeed. If someone's trying to understand the recipe for confidence, it implies there are only two routes: either be good enough to hit the target or – if that seems a bit tricky – aim for something less.

For anyone who is aspirational, there's a parallel set of everyday messaging that encourages them to leave their comfort zone. Aspiration means aiming for things that are difficult and not settling for something that doesn't take much sweat. For an aspirational student, settling for something easily achievable doesn't really work as a confidence boost: it doesn't seem valuable enough to generate self-worth. It's a bit like telling a worried maths A level student to have self-belief because they can now do their five times table mistake-free. The aspirational student – by definition – wants to succeed in areas where success is not yet signed and sealed.

For students who are aiming for things that are out of their comfort zone, the *believe in yourself, you've got this* message doesn't really work. It's false comfort: if the student is stretching themselves, by definition their grades are not a given: they haven't *got them* yet at all.

The much stronger version of confidence is the belief that mistakes can be handled. I think about my early, unconfident days in the classroom and I think about the difference now. There's still a risk that I've messed up the photocopying, or that I forgot to set the homework properly, or that I've lost my board pen. I still make frequent mistakes when I'm teaching. The difference is that I've learned how to deal with these. After 20 years in the classroom I've learned to accept them; I still don't like making mistakes but they don't phase me in the same way.

If students equate confidence with getting things right, then the risk of getting things wrong will reduce their confidence. Our simplifying, generalising brains take these as mirror-image counterparts: *the better I do, the more confident I'll be* is equated to the *less well I think I'll do, the less confident I should feel*; this in turn warps into if *I'm feeling unconfident, it's a sign it'll go badly*.

Unfortunately for students, this gives rise to a vicious circle: as soon as they believe that getting things right is the route to the confidence super-power, the desire to avoid getting things wrong increases. But if real confidence rests in knowing that mistakes can be handled, then mistakes are an essential building block: our students need *mistake expertise*.

If that tag line seems surprising, you can take it as evidence of how mistake-resistant we've become. There's a disconnect here between our wish that young people become confident and our unwillingness to give them the opportunity to develop this for real. If we throw resilience into the mix, the same conclusion appears: resilience is a bounce-back. It's clearly impossible to develop it without something to bounce back from.

> I talk to the students about intelligence versus wisdom: I ask them, who is more intelligent – them or me? They always say it'll be me, but I tell them, no, it's them: they're giving more time to this than I am, they've got the book-smarts on this because they're right in it. But I tell them I'm more wise because I've done it for

Strategies to use (classroom focus): Developing mistake expertise

When do school students get to evaluate how good they are at making mistakes? Would they even know what that means? Does it mean the more mistakes they make, the better? Surely not…?

Mistake expertise means skill in handling mistakes: it's not about the number of mistakes someone made, it's about how they responded to those mistakes. If teenagers know they have mistake expertise, then the prospect of mistakes becomes far less daunting. The concept of mistake expertise helps students understand that *yes, no one likes making a mistake, yes, it always feels a bit sour*, but here is the route for learning how to navigate mistakes in the most constructive way possible. If students can look back on moments at school and see how their mistake expertise has developed, they are far less likely to be fearful about mistakes in the future.

It's worth unpacking the ingredients that develop mistake expertise. The table below offers a possible way to evaluate skills related to mistake-making. It's a useful structure to enable students to reflect on how they are responding to mistakes. The questions are suggestions for how to prompt the thinking that will help students be reflective.

A worksheet based on the table is also available as an online resource for download at bloomsbury.pub/exam-stress.

Mistake-expertise score card: *think of a recent mistake…*	Score out of 10
1. **Interest:** *Were you interested in this mistake? Did you pause to notice it and think about what it showed you about what you understood then and what you now understand about how to do something differently?*	
2. **Perspective:** *Did you pause to make sure you put the mistake into perspective? How important was it really? It might have felt like a big thing at the time, but what was its long-term impact? Overall, does it rank as major, medium or minor? Did it feel that way at the time?*	

Mistake-expertise score card: *think of a recent mistake...*	Score out of 10
3. **Realism:** *Is your belief about how much you wanted to get right realistic? What counted as good enough in this context? Did this mistake take you below this line or not? Realistically, how many mistakes were likely at this stage? Think about the amount of time that was realistic to spend on the work: how likely were mistakes in this context?*	
4. **Self-compassion and tolerance:** *No one likes making mistakes. Did it feel rough? Does it still feel rough? Did you give yourself time to acknowledge this feeling? Were you able to tolerate the feeling, remembering that these feelings are inevitable sometimes, we need to get used to them and remember that they pass?*	

Balance

A major theme within this book has been the stress that comes with making choices. As Chapter 2 discussed, with choice comes responsibility and with responsibility comes the risk of self-blame. As teenagers get older, making choices becomes more complicated: by the time they are in Year 13, part of this complication is the difficulty of turning things down.

In the early stages of school-based choice-making, the choices are comparatively straightforward. *Would you like to join the fitness club? Say yes if you'd like to, no if you wouldn't.* Sometimes students are faced with a clash where they have to choose between two things they'd like to do, but most of the time they don't have to carry the regret of turning something down. For GCSE subjects, the choosing-not-to aspect of choice-making is a bit more obvious. Some students feel a bit sad to give a subject up, but once Year 10 gets going it's rare to find a student still gutted about the fact they couldn't squeeze an extra subject in as well.

In sixth form and in the move to life beyond school, the choice matrix becomes more complicated because the regret of not doing something becomes more present. Students have more moments when they have to choose either A or B because it's not possible to do both: get a part-time job or do homework? Support their families in the caring responsibilities at home or hang out with friends? Go to university or start earning money right away? Dealing with the feelings surrounding what you chose not to do or had to turn down can be complex. I don't think anyone goes through their adult life without a fair few moments of *I wish I could have done that as well* regret.

As Chapter 9 discussed, we often present choice-making as a positive thing – and it is – but it's not positive and positive alone. Much of this book has advocated for helping young people understand nuance; part of the nuance in choice-making is that being ready to choose not to do something is just as important as saying *yes* and adding an extra thing in.

Work–life balance: this is one of the most familiar bits of wellbeing advice around but, conceptually, balance only works on a one-in, one-out basis. If I want to add a bit more work in, then I have to realise that the balance will shift unless I take something out elsewhere. This is easier said than done, but the sooner someone gets used to asking *what will I stop doing in order to start doing something else*, the more likely it is that they will be able to maintain a balance that works for them.

For teenagers today, the work–life balance principle becomes more complicated because social media and ever-present phones create a world where work and life run concurrently, creating blended experiences where students are messaging friends while writing an essay or checking notifications during the school day. The pie-chart for balance becomes a bit harder to see because the segments overlap. When teenagers leave school and move into an adult world where balance is not engineered via the timetable of the school day, it's an even greater challenge. As the student below comments, creating boundaries in order to allocate time in a balanced way isn't easy, but – as is so often the case – acknowledging the difficulty is the first step to making the situation more manageable.

> I think social media does impact how much time you have, how busy you are to an extent. It's kind of fine while everything's fine in terms of friends and stuff – then it's positive – it's a way you can relax. As soon as problems begin, then it does become quite taxing – the problems come home with you, there's no escape from it. You want to seem like you're available to your friends so that people don't think you're a horrible person. Most people don't manage to set boundaries. I had a friend who had really serious screen-time apps to put boundaries in. I respected her but it was also really hard because her WhatsApp limit would kick in and she'd disappear from the conversation. I'd feel that I wanted to talk to her but then she wasn't there. It's really hard to set flexible boundaries – I don't think it's possible really.
>
> University student

Strategies to use (year-group focus): Clarifying the balance

I often say to students *look, the hard fact is that time is finite: there are only so many hours in the day. You have to make choices about how much time to give something. You need to remember that if you give time to one thing, you are not giving time to something else.*

Finding a balance is only possible if someone takes stock of their current time allocations and asks whether they are spending their time in the way that works best for them. This is a very personal thing; it rests on individual values and priorities. It's a natural next step from the values work suggested in Chapter 9.

The table below gives a way to think through this in a structured way. It's the sort of thing that can be done during form time or as part of a PSHE programme. The number of rows are, of course, optional, depending on the number of different things a student wants to give time to.

The following table is also available as an online resource for download at bloomsbury.pub/exam-stress.

- **Step 1:** Use the first column to list the different things you want to give your time to (e.g. friends, schoolwork, fitness, family, part-time job). Write one thing in each row.
- **Step 2:** Score each of these things out of 10, based on how important they are to you.
- **Step 3:** Roughly what percentage of your free time do you give to each of these things?
- **Step 4:** Are your time allocations in line with your values? If not, circle the things that need to be reduced in order to create time for the things that mean more to you.

Activities	Importance (out of 10)	Time (%)

Step 4 is where finding a balance begins, because it focuses on the idea of reducing one thing as a necessary part of saying *yes* to something else. It also helps to make it easier to turn something down, because it puts the *if only I could do this too* regret into the context of the bigger picture. It allows someone to say *yes, OK, I could have given more time to football training, but I chose not to because I knew that, for me, having a part-time job was more important. I had to make choices and this was the best balance for me.*

> *At university, the biggest thing that helps is having a really set work–life balance, e.g. saying at 6pm onwards I'm stopping. This really helps you not feel guilty about not working. Having something that isn't exams is really important – being about to clock-off is really helpful. I had a tutor in my first year who told me that and it made a big difference.*
>
> University student

Adaptability

> *It feels very daunting and you're constantly questioning* am I good enough, will this be OK? *You don't get that answer until results day and that's a long time afterwards. The wait after the exams is maybe more scary – you're just sitting around waiting, there's endless time until results day – nothing to distract you.*
>
> University student

> *There was a lot more stress going round at A level. I think this is because A levels matter more – you need to get good grades because you want to go to university. Universities look at GCSE grades but not that much. GCSE grades – they don't unlock the next stage in the same way that A levels do.*
>
> University student

> *In the summer term of Year 13 there's a level of superficial relief that exams are taking place, the to-do list is ticking down. But it's the implications of knowing how they think they have done, this adds a larger beast of pressure for what they think they must get. They really focus on whether they think they have the A* or not. This is a powerful thing if you have A*s in the university offers. As a qualifying bar it becomes a bigger deal when they know it impacts the grade*

that they need. This is particularly acute in maths etc., where they really can work out how many marks they've got.

Housemaster

We can't guarantee the future. This has been a core principle within this book. Nervousness about outcomes will always exist because there's always a degree of uncertainty there, even if the preparation has been as thorough and careful as possible. The more rigid the desired outcome is, the greater the likely unease. As the final exams approach, things can ramp up: university or next-phase offers often rest on a fixed set of conditions. If things go wrong, there's an obvious consequence.

If confidence rests in knowing that mistakes can be handled, then a subset of confidence is knowing that there's enough adaptability in place to recalibrate around mistakes or surprising outcomes.

Invest in the Plan B: this advice is equivalent to saying *be ready to recalibrate, practise thinking yourself into different situations and seeing the positive potential within them*. It's useful for students to think about the importance of agility as a life skill: *be ready to adapt, be agile enough to flex in line with the curve-balls that might come your way.*

As children grow up, sometimes they do not realise how agile and adaptable they are. Childhood and adolescence is a constant process of adapting to a new life phase, but these changes take place incrementally, making them harder to notice. Children often don't pause to reflect on the skills they've already acquired in handling change. Think of the surprise children experience when they return to a familiar place from their past and find themselves bigger: thinking retrospectively about what they've done in the past helps them see more clearly what they can do now.

👥 Strategies to use (year-group focus): Noticing adaptability

The key thing for teenagers to notice is that adaptability is something they have already demonstrated; realising this will help them feel more confident in their ability to manage the changes that the future will inevitably bring.

The questions below are a way to shape a retrospective thought-piece; they are similar to the forward-facing reflection outlined in Chapter 9 as a way to ease the transition into sixth form. The most important takeaway from this exercise is that it reminds students to think about the changes they have already made; it also reminds them that unfamiliar situations often feel uncomfortable, but this is a feeling that passes.

The following exercise is also available as an online resource for download at bloomsbury.pub/exam-stress.

Thinking back

This is an exercise to help you notice how adaptable you've learned to be. In your time at school, you've had to adapt to different situations. We're going to take some time to notice this. I'm going to ask you to write your thoughts down; you won't have to share these with anyone. This is just an opportunity for you to see your own skill set and experience so that you can recognise its value.

Think back to starting Year 7

- *Can you remember your first day or week? How did it feel?*
- *By the end of Year 7, what had changed? What had you started to do differently?*
- *What advice would you give to your Year 7-self to help them adapt?*

Think back to starting Year 12

- *Was this easier or harder than starting Year 7? Why?*
- *When did Year 12 start to feel normal? Was this just a matter of getting used to it, or was there something you did that eased things along?*
- *Think about the difference between you now and then; what does this show about how you've adapted to a different environment?*

Think about other changes in your life

- *What helped you adapt to these?*
- *Think about changes in the future: what would you like to remember to help you adapt to these?*

Self-compassion

One thing I'd want teachers to know is that if you see someone is stressed, don't tell them it's not worth being stressed about – telling them that is so unhelpful.

University student

Don't tell them it's not worth being stressed about: this was an idea that came through in many of the conversations I had with students. If students are stressed, it is because they are worried that something they care about is going to go badly. Telling them it's not worth caring about in the first place devalues what they are feeling; it devalues something that really matters to them.

Nobody would choose to be stressed about an exam, and it's natural for a teenager to feel angry that they are feeling this way. This anger can easily turn inwards, especially if they're hearing that *there's no need to feel this stressed*. Anger then makes the feelings harder to handle. This is where self-compassion comes in: teenagers need to remember that they feel stressed partly because they care. Caring about doing well is a good thing: yes, stress is its uncomfortable off-shoot, but caring about outcomes is a characteristic that's worth valuing.

Self-compassion: what does this mean? The Latin roots of the word *compassion* mean being there in the feeling, alongside it. Compassion is something we usually think of showing to others, but it works internally too. The exam-stressed student who tries to fight against their unease, who tries to push it away by working even harder or giving up caring altogether, is a student who will find that feeling harder to manage. Self-compassion means finding a way to accept that feeling stressed is not a fault in the emotional hardware.

Take the rough with the smooth: this is such good advice, but it only works if teenagers remember that the rough goes along with the smooth – there's no magic way to access smooth only. Caring about outcomes, being motivated, moving out of the comfort zone - these are all good things, but they all bring rougher aspects along with them too. *Yes, you're worried: I can help you with this. I can help you understand that this is natural, I can help you think about the balance that will help keep this outcome in perspective. I can help you remember that whatever outcome you get will be manageable and offer its own opportunities. But there'll be a bit of this feeling there all the same: it's there because you care and that's a good thing.*

Strategies to use (individual focus): Value where it comes from

All the other strategies in this book are designed to be used with a whole group at a time: in the classroom, during form time, year-group assemblies, family messaging. We all know, though, that some of the most important work we do is in the one-to-ones. If you are in a one-to-one conversation with a student because they have hit a limit with their stress, it is sometimes worth asking them *do you wish you could turn it off, get rid of this feeling altogether?* The answer will probably be yes. *OK, I understand that – life would be much easier without it. But what would you have to stop caring about first in order to not feel this way?*

It's worth giving space for this answer. When you think the student has had enough time to remember why they care about these outcomes in the first place, it can be helpful to ask them, *do you really want to stop caring about this? The reasons you care – these are good reasons, you can feel proud of the values that you have. This feeling, it doesn't make you feel good, but it's connected to something important to you. It's worth remembering this.*

It can be surprisingly reassuring for a child to hear this; it's worth thinking about why this is the case. When a small child cries, the reflex response is *what's wrong?* This can embed the idea that difficult feelings happen *because* something is wrong. Sometimes children need our help in remembering that sometimes they'll feel this way even if they are doing it right.

> *When I was in secondary school, we had a new headmaster: he spoke about a growth mindset. This was one of the most unhelpful things anyone has ever said to me. It predicated the idea that if you don't automatically feel comfortable, then you have a fixed mindset, not a growth mindset. It implied that if you were feeling stressed, it was an attitude problem with you. It would have been much more helpful to hear, OK, I understand your stress, it's OK to be stressed, it's understandable. Hearing this – and getting practical tips about stopping working – this would have been much better.*
>
> University student

Areas for action

In the classroom

- Are we creating opportunities for students to upskill in mistake expertise?

As a year group

- Are we offering the opportunity for students to think about how to find a balance that works for them?
- Are we helping students notice how adaptable they can be?

In one-to-one conversations

- Are we helping teenagers understand that difficult feelings often come from a good place?

Endnote

When I was interviewing people for this book, at the end of the interview I'd usually ask, *if you could only say one thing about exam stress, what would it be and who would you say it to?*

What one thing would I say? I'd have to make a bid for two: to the teachers, support staff and mental health practitioners who work with teenagers, I'd say that I think you do an amazing job. In every interview I did, I was struck by the care, compassion and skill which is woven into everyday life in schools. Your roles are often underpaid, overworked and undervalued. You deal every day with situations that are difficult, complex and changeable: children need people like you in their lives.

To the students at school who are feeling the exam stress, I'd say this: *Tell me more. Tell me how it feels. Let me try to understand what it's like for you right now. Let me listen. Once you are sure that I have heard you, then let's think about how we can help.*

Bibliography

Works directly referred to in the text are listed in bold below.

Atkinson, C., Brown, K.-A. and Soares, D. (2019), 'What can schools do about examination and test anxiety'. The Ofqual Blog Available at: https://ofqual.blog.gov.uk/2019/03/15/what-can-schools-do-about-examination-and- test-anxiety

BBC Bitesize (2003), '5 tips to help you relieve stress in the run-up to exams'. Available at: www.bbc.co.uk/bitesize/articles/z8dw239

Biddle, L., Gunnell, D., Sharp, D. and Donovan, J. L. (2004), 'Factors influencing help seeking in mentally distressed young adults: A cross-sectional survey', *British Journal of General Practice*, 54, (501), 248–253.

Blakemore, S.-J. (2018), *Inventing Ourselves: The Secret Life of the Teenage Brain*. London: Penguin Random House.

Brown, B. (2021), *Atlas of the Heart: Mapping Meaningful Connection and the Language of Human Experience*. London: Vermilion.

Carver, C. S. and Scheier, M. F. (2005), 'Engagement, disengagement, coping and catastrophe', in A. Elliot and C. Dweck (eds), *Handbook of Competence and Motivation*. New York: Guildford Publications, pp. 527–547.

Cassady, J. C. (2009), *Anxiety in Schools: The Causes, Consequences, and Solutions for Academic Anxieties*. New York: Peter Lang Inc. International Academic Publishers.

Childline (2019), 'Childline annual review 2018/2019'. Available at: https://learning.nspcc.org.uk/research-resources/childline-annual-review#heading-top

Childline (2023), 'How to deal with exam stress'. Available at: www.childline.org.uk/info-advice/school-college-and-work/school-college/tackling-exam-season

Children's Commissioner (2024), 'Children's mental health services 2022–2023'. Available at: www.childrenscommissioner.gov.uk/resource/childrens-mental-health-services-2022-23

Csikszentmihalyi, M. (1975), *Beyond Boredom and Anxiety*. San Francisco: Jossey-Bass Publishers.

Culler, R. E. and Holohan, C. J. (1980), 'Test anxiety and academic performance: The effects of study-related behaviours', *Journal of Educational Psychology*, 72, 16–26.

Davis, H. A., DiStefano, C. and Schutz, P. A. (2008), 'Identifying patterns of appraising tests in first-year college students: Implications for anxiety and emotion regulation during test taking', *Journal of Educational Psychology*, 100, 942–960.

DfE (2019), 'Achievement of 15-year-olds in England: PISA 2018 results: Executive summary'. Available at: https://assets.publishing.service.gov.uk/media/5f20292e8fa8f57ac3af2d11/PISA_2018_England_Exec_summary.pdf

Elliot, A. and Dweck, C. (eds), *Handbook of Competence and Motivation*. New York: Guildford Publications.

Family Lives (2023), 'Exam stress'. Available at: www.familylives.org.uk/advice/teenagers/school-learning/exam-stress

Gladwell, M. (2009), *Outliers: The Story of Success*. London: Penguin Random House.

Haidt, J. (2024), *The Anxious Generation*. London: Allen Lane.

Hembree, R. (1988), 'Correlates, causes, and treatment of test anxiety', *Review of Educational Research*, 58, 47–77.

Howard, E. (2020), 'A review of the literature concerning anxiety for educational assessments'. Available at: gov.uk/government/publications/a-review-of-the-literature-on- anxiety-for-educational-assessments

Huberty, T. J. and Dick, A. C. (2006), 'Performance and test anxiety', in G. Bear and K. Minke (eds), *Children's Needs* (3rd edn). Bethesda, MD: National Association of School Psychologists, pp. 281–291.

Kahneman, D. (2012), *Thinking, Fast and Slow*. London: Penguin Random House.

Mental Health Foundation (2024), '60% of young people unable to cope due to pressure to succeed'. Available at: www.mentalhealth.org.uk/about-us/news/60-young-people-unable-cope-due-pressure-succeed

Mind (2023), '14 ways to beat exam stress'. Available at: www.mind.org.uk/information-support/your- stories/14-ways-to-beat-exam-stress/#.XI9aZtr7R9A

Morgan, N. (2013), *Blame My Brain: The Amazing Teenage Brain Revealed*. London: Walker Books.

Morgan, N. (2018), *The Teenage Guide to Life Online*. London: Walker Books.

Murphy, L. (2022), 'Not working: Exploring changing trends in youth worklessness in the UK, from the 1990s to the Covid-19 pandemic'. Resolution Foundation. Available at: www.resolutionfoundation.org/app/uploads/2022/06/Not-working.pdf

Music, G. (2024), *Nurturing Natures: Attachment and Children's Emotional, Sociocultural and Brain Development*. Abingdon: Routledge.

NHS England (2018), 'Mental health of children and young people in England, 2017'. Available at: https://digital.nhs.uk/data-and-information/publications/statistical/mental-health-of-children-and-young-people-in-england/2017/2017

NHS England (2022), 'Mental health of children and young people in England, 2022'. Available at: https://digital.nhs.uk/data-and-information/publications/statistical/mental-health-of-children-and-young-people-in-england/2022-follow-up-to-the-2017-survey

NHS England (2023), 'Help your child beat exam stress'. Available at: www.nhs.uk/conditions/stress-anxiety-depression/coping-with-exam-stress

OECD (2017), *PISA 2015 Results (Volume III): Students' Well-Being*. Paris: OECD Publishing.

OECD (2019a), *PISA 2018 Results (Volume III): What School Life Means for Students' Lives*. Paris: OECD Publishing.

OECD (2019b), *PISA 2018 Insights and Interpretations*. Paris: OECD Publishing.

OECD (2023a), *PISA 2022 Insights and Interpretations*. Paris: OECD Publishing.

OECD (2023b), *PISA 2022 Results (Volume I): The State of Learning and Equity in Education*. Paris: OECD Publishing.

OECD (2024), *The PISA Happy Life Dashboard: Visualising Key Indicators on Student Well-Being from the PISA Survey*. Paris: OECD Publishing.

Ofqual (2023), 'Coping with exam pressure – a guide for students'. Available at: www.gov.uk/government/publications/coping-with-exam-pressure-a-guide-for-students/coping-with-exam-pressure-a-guide-for-students

Public Health England (2016), 'The mental health of children and young people in England'. Available at: https://assets.publishing.service.gov.uk/media/5a80c3e24 0f0b62305b8d06c/Mental_health_of_children_in_England.pdf

Richardson, P. J. and Boyd, R. (2004), *Not by Genes Alone: How Culture Transformed Human Evolution*. Chicago: University of Chicago Press.

Rickwood, D., Deane, F. P., Wilson, C. J. and Ciarrochi, J. (2005), 'Young people's help- seeking for mental health problems', *Australian e-journal for the Advancement of Mental Health*, 4, (3), 218–251.

Ricky, E. (2000), *Ideas in Psychoanalysis: Anxiety*. Cambridge: Icon Books.

Rosenshine, B. (2010), *Principles of Instruction*. London: International Academy of Education.

Salaheddin, K. and Mason, B. (2016), 'Identifying barriers to mental health help-seeking among young adults in the UK: A cross-sectional survey', *British Journal of General Practice*, 66, (651), 686–692.

Schuler, P. A. (2000), 'Perfectionism in the gifted adolescent', *Journal of Secondary Gifted Education*, 11, 183–196.

Sharfran, R., Egan, S. and Tracey, W. (2018), *Overcoming Perfectionism: A Self-Help Guide Using Scientifically Supported Cognitive Behavioural Techniques* (2nd edn). London: Robinson.

Sherrington, T. (2019), *Rosenshine's Principles in Action*. Woodbridge: John Catt Educational.

Siegel, D. J. (2021), *Brainstorm: The Power and Purpose of the Teenage Brain*. London: Scribe.

Smith, Dr J. (2022), *Why has Nobody Told me this Before?* London: Penguin Michael Joseph.

Spielberger, C. D. (1973), *Manual for the State-Trait Anxiety Inventory for Children*. Palo Alto, CA: Consulting Psychologists Press.

Student Minds (2024), 'Exam stress'. Available at: www.studentminds.org.uk/examstress.html

Taleb, N. (2010), *The Black Swan: The Impact of the Highly Improbable*. London: Penguin Random House.

Taleb, N. (2012), *Antifragile: Things That Gain from Disorder*. London: Penguin Random House.

Teenagers Translated (2024), 'Managing exam stress'. Available at: www.teenagerstranslated.co.uk/exam-stress.php

The Student Room (2024), 'Your guide to handling revision and exam stress'. Available at: www.thestudentroom.co.uk/revision/exams/dealing-with-exam-stress

Turkle, S. (2015), *Reclaiming Conversation: The Power of Talk in a Digital Age*. London: Penguin Random House.

van der Kolk, B. (2014), *The Body Keeps the Score*. London: Penguin Random House.

Vogels, E. A., Gelles-Watnic, R. and Massarat, N. (2022), 'Teens, social media and technology 2022'. Available at: www.pewresearch.org/Internet/2022/08/10/teens-social-media-and- technology-2022

Wang, Q., Pomeranta, E. M. and Chen, H. (2007), 'The role of parents' control in early adolescents' psychological functioning: A longitudinal investigation in the United States and China', *Child Development*, 78, (5), 1592–1610.

Young Minds (2024), 'How to help your child manage exam stress'. Available at: https://youngminds.org.uk/blog/exam-results-stress-advice-for-parents

Zeidner, M. and Matthews, G. (2005), 'Evaluation anxiety: Current theory and research', in A. J. Elliot and C. S. Dweck (eds), '*Handbook of Competence and Motivation*'. New York: Guildford Press, pp. 141–163.

Index

Index

Notes: The student perspective

- In your context, what are the key things that create exam stress for your students?

- In your context, what are the most useful things for your students to hear?

Notes: Preparing for exams

- In your context, how can you help your students feel their revision plan is sensible and manageable?

Notes: Thinking beyond the exams

- In your context, what would you like your students to take with them as well as their grades?

A Parent's Guide to Exam Stress:
Practical, positive ways to support your child for GCSEs, A levels and other school assessments

The ultimate guide to why so many children experience problematic levels of stress at school today, and what we – as parents – can do to understand and support them at home.

Katharine Radice draws on her training in child and adolescent development and 20+ years teaching in the classroom to provide you with practical advice, valuable insights and effective strategies to support your child through exams and assessments from KS3 to A level.

Contents

Available at www.bloomsbury.com